CUTTING THROUGH

PRAISE

"Having a process makes a difference. No matter how effective your personality and ability to motivate people may be, it's not enough. HPMS enabled me to combine effective communication/motivation with a process that keeps an organization focused on the right things. With focus and organizational alignment productivity soars!!!"
Tom Frinzi|Chief Commercial Officer of Bausch + Lomb, President of WaveTec Vision, President of Johnson & Johnson Vision

"We use HPMS in all of our businesses, it has been the key to clear communication, clear goals, happy employees, and is a big reason I love Mondays!"
John Berdahl, MD|Vance Thompson Vision, Equinox Ophthalmic, Melt Pharmaceuticals, ExpertOpinion.md

"Our team first deployed the HPMS system with Bernie's guidance in 2011 at Spectranetics. The clarity and alignment that the process drove yielded world class WTR from teammates and customers, and shareholder value went from ~$170m to $2.2b in six years. I strongly recommend Bernie and HPMS!"
Scott Drake|President and CEO of Spectranetics, President and CEO of ViewRay

"Had the great fortune to learn the HPMS process at ILSE under the tutelage of Bob Palmisano and Bernie Haffey. An individual transformation truly happened and subsequently fueled multiple business successes over the following 18 years. I could not envision a life without the guidance, clarity and confidence that HPMS provides as a business leader. Thank you Bob, Bernie and of course Dick Palermo."
Eric Weinberg |Chief Commercial Officer of IntraLase, LenSx, RxSight

"Why are some executives, coaches, leaders successful time after time? Why do some leaders seem to come out on top time after time? Why do some leaders seem to come out on top regardless of personnel, market or environmental factors beyond their control? Bernie Haffey **unlocks the complexity of high performance** by teaching what these great leaders know. I strongly encourage any leader of any organization to invest the time to learn more about Haffey's High Performance Management System."
J Andy Corley|President and CEO of eyeonics, President of Bausch + Lomb, Flying L Partners

"If you want to personally perform at a higher level, or lead your team to do the same, read Cutting Through! Whether to refresh your own performance, or to instill HPMS in your business, Cutting Through is a practical, relevant and action packed read that inspires ideas with every chapter and example".
Stacy Enxing Seng | President of ev3, President of Covidien, Venture Partner of Lightstone Ventures

"One of our Board members, Bess Weatherman, introduced me to the HPMS and Bernie Haffey, and I've never looked back. The common-sense nature of the system is very appealing to me, as is the simplicity. Focus on the Vital Few is a game changer."
Joe Army | President and CEO of Vapotherm

"HPMS is my business religion."
 Lance Berry| Chief Financial and Operations Officer of Wright Medical, Director of Vapotherm, Inc., Director of Priveterra Acquisition Corp.

"I've worked with Bernie at two different companies. After my first experience with HPMS, I quickly engaged Haffey & Co when I assumed a new CEO role in order to create strategic focus and organizational buy-in for the path forward. HPMS is a really

powerful tool and can help ensure everyone understands the priorities, what the organization stands for and what they need to do every day in order for the company to be successful."
Will McGuire | President and CEO of Second Sight Medical Products, President and CEO of Ra Medical Systems

"I have used Bernie Haffey and his management system and consulting advice for two companies I was CEO of with excellent results, his book is invaluable to a leader in any position where results are."
Randy Alexander | President and CEO of Intramedics Intraocular, President and CEO of ReVision Optics

"The business concepts Mr. Haffey eloquently brings to life in this important book can be counted on to bring discipline, clarity and alignment to even the most complex organizations. Good results inevitably follow."
Jim Lightman|General Counsel of Summit Technology, IntraLase, Wright Medical and Vapotherm

"Implementing the High Performance Management System at our practice has proved to be a game changer."
Vance Thompson MD|Founder of Vance Thompson Vision

"I have been an HPMS advocate since Bernie trained us in the process back in 2008. Since then, with Bernie's coaching, we have trained businesses that are now cumulatively doing more than $8B combined annually. While it looks deceptively easy (and much of it is), the real challenges (and extreme rewards) are in: insisting on breakthrough change, on prioritizing and choosing the vital few (and truly defunding the lower priorities allowing the vital few to flourish), and staffing the vital few with your "A" team. These tasks can be much harder than they seem - but this book can continue to remind you, guide you, and steel your resolve through this transformation. It is worth it!"
Earl Slee|VP Research and Technology at ev3, Covidien and Medtronic

"Many will have the temptation to "improve" the HPMS process early in the implementation phase. In actuality, the organization is attempting to change the process to match its current state, as opposed to implementing a tried and true process and changing its way of doing business. I would encourage leaders to implement the HPMS process in its current form. It can take up to two years for the processes to seep into the organization's DNA, but once they do, the velocity of change in the organization will increase dramatically. Bernie and team help organizations bring this to life."
Shar Matin|COO of Spectranetics, COO of ViewRay, President and CEO of Cordis Corporation

"The HPMS process outlined in Cutting Through worked for me in both the private equity and public company setting. There is no better way to align the board, employees, customers, and share-holders on the mission, vision, and strategy for a company. I experienced dramatic shifts in culture enabling breakthrough achievements. Employees come away with greater problem solving capacity, and the ability to shift and modify strategy at the pace required in today's business environment."
Joe Woody|Global President of Covidien, President and CEO of Acelity, President and CEO of Avanos

"If you want to transform your organization and get the very best out of the resources you have, then pay attention to Cutting Through. This is not an academic exercise. So many books these days are written too far from where the work is really done. Cutting Through provides you the practical tools and systems you need to consistently deliver. Don't make it more complicated that it is. Pick up the book and implement it right away. And just when it starts to get hard, keep going… that's when you know you're starting to change your business forever."
Joe Wishon|Business Process Program Director of Medtronic

"HPMS frees up great minds to think strategically since the process keeps problems transparent and the trains running on time with much less effort!"
Jonathan Talamo MD| Mass General Hospital, Mass Eye and Ear, Harvard Medical School, CMO of Ocular Therapeutix, CMO of Johnson&Johnson Vision

"An extraordinary collection of insight, know-how and practical application to take your management system into the next decade!"
Orad Elkayam|Founder of Mogi Group

"Haffey's book is a cut-and-dry blueprint on how to master your business processes, optimize workload efficiency and ensure that everyone is rowing in the same direction, towards the same end goal. A fantastic collection of research, theory, and practical strategy."
Steve Ferreira |Founder and CEO of Ocean Audit

"If you have an inkling that your system processes, company culture or internal output efficiency is not operating at the level of which it is capable, Bernie Haffey would probably agree with you. Luckily, Cutting Through offers a structured approach to exit out of the lethal disease that is poor management systems."
Sid Mohasseb|Transformational and Motivational Speaker, and bestselling author of *You Are Not Them!: The Authentic Entrepreneur's Way*

"If you were to condense thirty years of leadership, business acumen and management theory, what you would be left with is nothing short of Bernie Haffey's Cutting Through."
Rick Orford|Co-Founder & Executive Producer at Travel Addicts Life, and bestselling author of *The Financially Independent Millennial*

"A deeply rich dive into the realm of management theory and processes, Haffey never forgets - even for a moment - it is people that drive company systems and people that make them successful."
Sanjay Jaybhay|Bestselling author of *Invest and Grow Rich*

CUTTING THROUGH

Your Company's High Performance Management System

BERNIE HAFFEY

Leaders
Press

Leaders
Press

ISBN 978-1-63735-023-2 (pbk)

ISBN 978-1-63735-022-5 (e-book)

SIMON &
SCHUSTER

Print Book Distributed by Simon & Schuster

1230 Avenue of the Americas

New York, NY 10020

Library of Congress Control Number: 2021905063

To my wife Alexandra and children Lila, Kane and Grady, who provided the loving and supportive environment to make this book possible.

TABLE OF CONTENTS

FOREWORD

Cutting Through: Your Company's High Performance Management System

by Bob Palmisano

I have had the pleasure of knowing Bernie Haffey since 1997 when he joined my executive team at Summit Technology, Inc.[1] We worked together again at IntraLase[2] from 2003 to 2007. In both cases, we created phenomenal shareholder value by applying equal and, in some cases, more emphasis on the leading indicators of customer and employee satisfaction through the High Performance Management System (HPMS).

I've also had the pleasure of working with Bernie as a principal management consultant at ev3 Inc. and at Wright Medical[3], where his facilitation and implementation skills were invaluable.

I have seen Bernie's knowledge and application of HPMS continually improve over our two-decade relationship and was further delighted that he decided to write this much-needed update on HPMS theory and implementation.

I thoroughly enjoyed my copy of *Cutting Through: Your Company's High Performance Management System* and feel you will too. I would recommend it to any organization or individual seeking to improve their individual leadership skills and the performance of their organizations.

If you practice what Bernie writes about in this text with "orthodoxy", I am certain that with time and persistence, you will achieve

---

[1] Sold to Alcon Labs for $972 million in 2000
[2] Sold to Advanced Medical Optics (AMO) for $808 million in 2007
[3] Sold to Stryker for $5.4 billion in 2020

world-class results I've enjoyed in several organizations committed to HPMS and its processes.

Once you fully understand and implement the elements of this book, you will, in the thinking of W. Edwards Deming, "be transformed" and unable to look at business in the same way. You will move from simply managing results toward the processes and methods needed to generate and continually improve them. As my mentor, the late Dick Palermo, said:

> "The customers benefit from it, the employees want it, and the financial health of an organization depends on it."

I hope you take the time to read and digest the contents of this invaluable book, and if you haven't already, begin implementing HPMS in your organization.

Robert Palmisano
Chairman and CEO
Priveterra Acquisition Corp.

THE HIGH PERFORMANCE
MANAGEMENT SYSTEM

Are you a newly appointed leader of an organization in need of transformational change, a leader of an organization at a growth inflection point, or a leader of an early stage company in need of a solid foundation? If so, this book is for you. This book is also useful for aspiring leaders and managers of any organization. Once you learn the principles in this book and apply them through our management system, you will be well on your way to a dramatically different business.

I know this because I have participated as an executive and a consultant in numerous successful business turnarounds. The material in this book came from decades of experience—the teachers, mentors, and leaders that came before me; and the countless practitioners who have helped advance our management science and system.

My Introduction To The High Performance Management System (Hpms)

In September 1997, I joined the turnaround management team at Summit Technology, Inc. led by CEO Robert "Bob" Palmisano. Prior to Summit, I earned an MBA from a top school then worked my way up from a Product Manager role at Hewlett-Packard Co. to Vice President, Sales and Marketing of Mentor Corp.'s ophthalmic surgical business. So, by the time I arrived at Summit, I felt I knew something about leadership and management. Palmisano and a former Xerox executive named Richard "Dick" Palermo, completely and permanently changed this perspective.

Summit Technology was a Boston-area developer, manufacturer, and marketer of excimer laser systems initially targeted at cardio-vascular disease. Under the brilliant technical leadership of founder and CEO David Muller, PhD, the company pivoted from cardio-vascular to ophthalmic application of excimer and, in 1995, was first to receive FDA approval for photorefractive keratectomy (PRK) to correct myopia (nearsightedness). With a US market of 110 million (220 million eyes), the market was enormous. Summit was also successful in executing a unique and potentially profitable business model where users would purchase the laser for $500,000 and pay a $250 per-eye patent license fee. The large potential market, attractive business model, and charismatic CEO allowed for a successful initial public offering (IPO) in 1996, raising over $100 million in additional capital.

The Summit Apex Excimer Laser

With the IPO came high expectations, as much as 4 million procedures per year, for the highly lucrative procedure fees. Due to typical market adoption factors, however, procedures in the first year fell well short of expectations with a modest fifty-five thousand eyes treated in 1996. Summit responded to the pressures of the public market expectations by pointing to their customers, largely solo ophthalmic surgeon practices, for the shortfall. This in turn led the company to open nineteen company-owned Centers of Excellence in direct competition with their initial customers. The initial customers responded with vitriol and anger. Instead of helping their customers grow their businesses, Summit had put itself into direct competition with them. To further compound the problem, Summit had taken its "eye off the ball" and allowed VISX, Inc., its West Coast rival, to surpass them in technology, FDA approvals, and market share. The combination of disappointed shareholders and angry customers led Summit's Board of Directors to replace Dr. Muller in 1997 with Robert Palmisano, formerly President of Bausch and Lomb's Eyewear Division.

Palmisano quickly initiated a turnaround plan, which included divestiture of the company-owned centers; new executive leadership in marketing and sales, finance, manufacturing operations, regulatory and clinical affairs, and legal; and a mantra to "mean more to our customers." I was fortunate to have been part of this team, starting in 1997 as Vice President of Marketing and Sales.

Palmisano also brought in Dick Palermo as our primary management consultant to assist us in adopting and implementing HPMS. Through this system, and a lot of hard work, we transformed Summit from a company with highly dissatisfied customers, unmotivated employees, and dissatisfied shareholders to a world-class entity in less than four years—culminating in a $972-million-dollar sale to Alcon Laboratories in 2000. This exit represented a nearly $900 million dollar increase in shareholder value—a result, I believe, which would not have been possible absent the choreography and discipline provided by HPMS.

I still recall Dick's introduction of the HPMS to our executive team at an offsite meeting in December 1997. He spoke about the teachings of W. Edwards Deming and Joseph Juran, about the importance of culture and employee engagement, the need to see your business as a system of connected processes, and about the importance of process and leading indicators over the management of results.

At the first intermission, I went up to Dick and said, "I don't know what the other functions are going to do, but effective today, this is how we are going to run Marketing and Sales." In Deming terms, I had been "transformed" as an individual, and it was discontinuous! Over the next few years, we transformed Summit and I never looked back.

The system also transformed me as a manager and leader. Since 2000, I've implemented HPMS as a manager and primary consultant in over forty organizations—from large multinational corporations to small start-ups—often witnessing the same transformational results we enjoyed at Summit.

CHAPTER 1

OUT OF THE JUNGLE

Through over twenty years of executive operating experience and ten years of management consulting experience in over forty organizations, I've seen a lot of business stories that are as dramatic as any Hollywood movie. Some movies are works of art, worthy of reflection and repeat views, while others are messy and ugly with content you'd rather forget. The common theme in the latter category is waste, or what our Lean colleagues would call *muda*, a Japanese word meaning "futility, uselessness, wastefulness."

While many manufacturing operations are effective at minimizing waste in transportation, inventory, motion, waiting, over processing, overproduction, and defects through proven quality principles and practices, an appreciation for and understanding of waste in management process in other key operations (e.g., Service, Sales, R&D, Finance, HR, etc.) is often lacking. In some cases, the amount of waste and absence of quality practice increases the further you move from the factory floor toward the boardroom. It breaks my heart to see it this way.

The four primary sources of management waste, in our experience, are:

1. Over-Management Of Results/Absence Of Clear Management Theory

The number one source of management waste comes from leaders and managers who, absent an understanding of management theory, focus solely on results—something they can see and understand. I am not saying you can manage a business absent appropriate management of results; rather that the best outcomes come from organizations that place a healthy emphasis on leading indicators through a connected, continuously improving management system.

To clarify this point, consider two car repair technicians, Max and Joe, each outfitted with the best tools for fixing cars. Max had mastered the theory of how a car operates, from the air/gas mixture to the exhaust, including a deep understanding of drivetrain and suspension mechanics. Joe possessed none of this theoretical knowledge or framework from which to diagnose and fix problems. I think it's pretty clear who you'd like to take your car to for repair!

The same analogy applies to leaders and managers, many times resulting in the misplaced belief that they can inspect quality into their processes and business outcomes. High-performance managers understand it's the processes and overall system that drive results and therefore shift their focus upstream to improve the way the work gets done.

2. Lack Of Alignment Between Functions, Departments, Teams, And Individuals

The second source of waste comes in the form of functions or departments optimizing their results, which in many cases comes at a significant cost to the whole. For example, an unbalanced system may burn out employees to meet certain customer, financial, or operational targets or constrain sales or operations based on financial goals. Organizations that can build and see the entire management system, along with their functional role to support it, can help lead and improve the system to the ultimate benefit of the organizations' customers, employees, and shareholders.

Consider an organization absent a system that practices a management by objectives (MBO) approach where each function, department, and individual set their own objectives. This results in too many measures and metrics, silos, poor communication and cooperation, a lack of understanding what is important, and a great deal of frustration in critical areas of work. A system view and systems thinking, where goals are set and aligned in a system, helps eliminate this enormous source of waste.

"When we create incentives to optimize parts of the system (low-cost supplier, sales incentives, evaluating return on investment for individual business units, etc.) the overall system is suboptimized. In order to achieve the best overall results, individual parts of the system may have to suffer in order to achieve the best overall result."

—W. Edwards Deming

3. Lack Of Focus And Associated Inability To Execute

Absent a system-wide view and process for agreeing on a set of a "Vital Few" priorities, organizations focus on doing too many things and quite often, none particularly well.

Let's use the analogy of a juggler to make this point. Early in my career, I was a pretty good juggler and kept getting more balls passed my way. Pretty soon, I was juggling too many balls and unable to concentrate on any of them in particular. Even more concerning is that when a juggler drops one ball, they drop all of the balls!

Through focus on a shorter list of vital priorities, your organization will be positioned to achieve breakthroughs in performance in selected areas instead of incremental across many.

The Juggler

4. A Penchant For Complexity

Coinciding with lack of focus is a penchant for complexity over simplicity. It's an unfortunate element of the human condition to add—to plans, processes, procedures and products—rather than subtract. The Amazon Management System recognizes this human element as entropy, a term from thermodynamics that reflects a system's tendency toward chaos. At Amazon, they abhor complexity and understand that, if left unattended, the total entropy or level of disorder will increase. They possess a "deliberate vigilance and institutional determination to fight entropy."

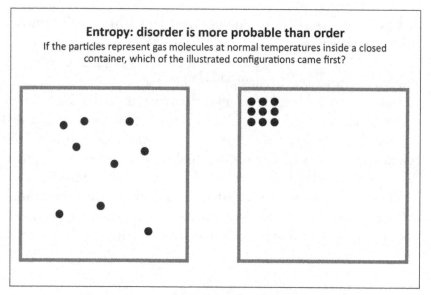

Entropy: disorder is more probable than order
If the particles represent gas molecules at normal temperatures inside a closed container, which of the illustrated configurations came first?

"Disorder is more probable than order."

Fortunately, there's a clear, simple, and logical way out of the jungle to world-class customer, employee, and financial results. Read on to learn how.

CHAPTER 2

THE SIX PILLARS OF THE HIGH PERFORMANCE MANAGEMENT SYSTEM

Principle 1—Driving Through A System

> "94% of problems in business are systems driven and only 6% are people driven."
>
> —W. Edwards Deming

If you peel back the curtain on nearly every leader who has had repeated success, you will find that their success is much less about the person and more about the system and processes they have deployed. In any organization, whether it consists of thirty people or 300,000, a leader can do only so much. They cannot follow every employee around and tell them what to do; rather they rely on common goals, behaviors, and a continuously improving management system. By building a system based on sound management theory, you make the business less dependent on you being in the office every hour of the day and create a foundation that can continuously improve.

Not convinced? One of the most successful US Football coaches in history, Nick Saban, is known for what he calls "The Process" which is a makeup of practices based on years of trial and error. At the core of "The Process" is a focus on continuous improvement and improvement in the consistency of results, which is what the term quality is all about! No one is above "The Process," and everyone knows what is expected of them and how to make decisions that fit his model success model.

The example above can be found in all reaches of life. This chapter will cover management theory and the father of quality, W. Edwards Deming, whose principles changed the course of history in manufacturing and modern business practices.

Principle 2—Building A Coalition

> "If you think you're a leader and you turn around and no one is following you, then you're simply out for a walk."
>
> —James M. Kouzes

Having the right people committed to your direction and system is critically important to the your company's success. Leaders who focus on building buy-in rather than force and authority tend to be more successful. Besides the energy drain associated with pushing people around, it also means that you alone have to maintain the company initiatives, inspect everyone's work, and be constantly vigilant about ensuring people are doing what you want. Most leaders simply don't have time for that level of micromanagement.

Building a successful team starts with finding a strong number two person committed to making your system a reality. By recruiting this critical person, you will have considerably improved your chances of success. You can then work on the third, fourth, etc. until the movement takes on a life of its own. Many of us have been in companies where this was not done well or are currently still there now. It doesn't feel great to work in that culture with rumblings about the system being a "flavor of the month," or "We'll do things differently in our department."

Everyone yearns to be part of a winning team. This chapter will go through the importance of building your core team and creating a movement that extends to every employee.

Principle 3—Affirming Your Direction And Culture

"Actual company values, as opposed to the nice sounding values, are shown by who gets rewarded, promoted, or let go."

—Reed Hastings, CEO of Netflix

Imagine learning how to play golf for the first time but not being taught where to hit the ball, how far to send it, how to swing the club, or the rules of play. Contrast that to someone who is given the green as a target, a distance to achieve, and some tips on how to swing the club. Who do you think would be more successful?

When working on a team in a business, everyone must see where they are going, what they are doing, and what behaviors are necessary for success. As with the golf student above, if a team isn't aligned, the odds of success are low. Everyone will do their best; however, absent an understanding of the goal and process to achieve it, best efforts are not enough.

By spending time to align the team with a compelling future, clarifying what each person does each day, and driving accountability for behaviors, odds of success are high. This goes through core elements for forming a Vision, Mission, and set of Shared Values for your team. Practical uses of these tools will be provided in this chapter.

Principle 4—Connecting With Your Key Stakeholders

"If you don't listen to your customers, someone else will."

—Sam Walton

Have you ever purchased a product only to realize that it was infuriating to use, and you returned it or threw it away? Have you ever worked for a company and could easily see how leadership was driving the company off a cliff? These disconnects are often the result of leadership insulating themselves from their customers, employees, or shareholders. These leadership teams are working hard but often not on the right tasks. They can be found sitting in boardrooms pondering why numbers on a spreadsheet are not trending in the right direction rather than connecting with what is vitally important to their success. As a result, their direct reports spend more time preparing presentations and creating new reports than doing value-added work.

It is essential to create channels to listen to and deeply understand your most important stakeholders: customers, employees, and shareholders. You must understand the top opportunities for company improvement, the strength of engagement with your company, and which parts of their experience need work. Customers are giving you a blueprint toward success—they are already buying your products and services and want it to be better! Your employees are the same. They spend more time with your company than with their friends and family. Give them a voice and allow them to help you make the company more competitive and attractive to top talent.

Understanding the needs and aspirations of your shareholders is also essential. While many think the obvious feedback is for you to make more money, you will find different opinions on opportunities. Understanding and acting on their expectations can help ensure you set the right expectations and move with the proper sense of urgency.

This chapter goes into methods for regularly collecting, analyzing and acting on your key stakeholder inputs. I also provide compelling examples describing how this practice can lead to breakthrough results.

Principle 5—Driving "Wicked" Strategic Clarity

> "People think focus means saying yes to the thing you've got to focus on. But that's not what it means at all. It means saying no to the hundred other good ideas that there are. You have to pick carefully."
>
> —Steve Jobs

Every company, team, and individual has a finite amount of time and resources. Numerous studies show that we are delusional as a species to think that we are good multitaskers. To pile on from there, we often underestimate the time and energy needed to complete large tasks. With those three factors at work, it's no surprise that most employees feel overworked, working from fire to fire in businesses and not making significant headway on their hopes and dreams.

Every employee and leader in an organization craves clarity, not just a task list but a no-kidding priority list of what is most important. Robust prioritization is not an easy task, and many ill-trained leaders continue to ask the organization to attempt to do everything, which invariably leads to failure.

Companies that drive clarity are more successful. As mentioned in chapter 1, a juggler with too many balls in the air doesn't just drop one; they drop them all. This chapter helps an organization get "wickedly" focused, covering how to identify and separate the "Vital Few" from the "useful many," a term coined decades ago by another legendary quality leader, Joseph Juran.

Principle 6—Flexing your Problem-Solving Muscles

> "The major problem we face is not any particular problem. It is the process we use to solve problems."
>
> —Steven Covey

Any company can put its best people together to solve one problem, but a week later, you may have ten more problems. By focusing on *how* you solve problems, you will build a muscle that will enable your company to overcome most hurdles.

The core of any problem-solving methodology is the scientific method—one of the most important methodologies invented by humanity. The continuous feedback loops associated with collecting information, deriving hypotheses, testing, and defining conclusions have progressed society. They are the reason there are planes in the sky, computers that help us communicate across the globe, and life-saving medications that improve and extend life.

Manufacturing is the crucible from which many great methodologies are born. If you've ever worked in a plant, you're aware there are problems that occur every day. While Lean and Six Sigma are too complicated and intimidating for most companies, there is no denying what the plan-do-check-act (PDCA) and define, measure, analyze, improve, and control (DMAIC) methodologies—both variants of the scientific method—have done for manufacturing companies who adopt them. Rather than drowning in problems, the best sites learn to chew through their issues in hours rather than days, allowing them to operate with lower customer complaints and improved margins.

This chapter goes into a simplified methodology you can implement in your organization and build the muscle that will allow you to quickly assess problems and forge a path to an exciting future.

Before Diving In

If you utilize these six principles, I am confident that your business will have a competitive advantage by aligning your people, processes, and resources through your company's High Performance Management System (HPMS). You'll find that management becomes more about designing and cultivating the way results are achieved rather than sitting in a boardroom reviewing spreadsheets that are the result of work done weeks or months earlier. The book will wrap up with a chapter describing practical steps for implementing these principles in your business.

CHAPTER 3

PRINCIPLE 1: DRIVING PERFORMANCE THROUGH A SYSTEM

Virtually all professions that allow our society to thrive rely on underlying principles and science to perform effectively. Doctors need to understand the underlying mechanisms of how our bodies function to treat our illnesses, engineers use thermodynamics to build turbofan engines, and auto mechanics use tried and true methods to troubleshoot and fix your car when it breaks. The frameworks create a foundation that can be improved over time. Yet, in management we rarely create strong or effective frameworks to drive success.

Often first-time leaders are simply thrown into the fire, many of whom were strong individual contributors, and learn through trial and error to figure out how to manage their teams effectively. This ideology is propagated to executive leaders, where some have zeroed in on their personal framework or system, while others may have succeeded through determination and personality alone. There is a better way to succeed, however, and it starts with understanding management theories that have been around for decades.

The Importance Of A Management System

Let's start with the importance of having a management system to govern teams and drive performance. The definition of a management system is a set of policies, processes, and procedures used by an organization to ensure it can fulfill the tasks required to achieve its objectives[4]. In plain English, it is the mechanism that helps teams organize and execute tasks.

To understand the purpose and benefit, imagine working for a company where no one knows the priorities, how they are progressing toward them, or the appropriate channels to escalate issues. Employees just choose projects they think are interesting or easy. In this example, the company would likely fail quickly as it ineffectively applies resources and cannot adapt in the everchanging business environment.

It's important to note that every company has a management system whether they know it or not. Many, however, are ill-defined or missing elements that could greatly improve the performance of the team. To help you develop your company's HPMS, I will cover the underlying theories that have been utilized successfully by management teams in all industries around the world.

W. Edwards Deming And Joseph Juran: The "DNA" Of HPMS

Many of the underlying quality principles and practices embedded in HPMS can be attributed to the work of W. Edwards Deming and Joseph Juran, pioneers in quality management. I liken their work to the "DNA" of HPMS. Deming's work in Japan, and later in the US, formed the basis for the Malcolm Baldrige National Quality Award in the US and the Deming Prize in Japan.

---

[4]   https://en.wikipedia.org/wiki/Management_system

Among Deming's numerous breakthroughs is the notion that product and service quality are the responsibility of management more so than the worker. It's therefore management's responsibility to:

- provide "constancy of purpose" including customer impact
- provide necessary training, coaching, tools, and resources
- provide appropriate reward and job recognition
- track and display key measures in associated places of work
- continuously improve and role model the system
- measure quality in the Voice of the Customer
- apply scientific thinking and methods to business problems and opportunities

Deming spent considerable time training people to understand that these seemingly simple practices, done well, lead to real business impact. His lectures, experiments, and trainings inspired countless people to become better and more productive leaders.

The Pareto Principle

Juran worked closely with Deming in Japan and throughout the world. While less well known than his counterpart, his observations and contributions were equally impactful. Trained as a chemical engineer, he was the first to apply the Pareto principle as a quality management tool, demonstrating that ≅20% of issues contributed to ≅80% of a problem or opportunity. The Pareto principle was named after Italian mathematician and economist Vilfredo Pareto and is considered to be one of the universally most powerful quality principles and tools—as such, I recommend you exercise it continuously. Building on this principle, Juran referred to the ≅20% as the "Vital Few" and the remaining ≅80% as the "trivial many", which he later modified to the "useful many." In our consulting practice and in HPMS, we further apply this principle to an organization's strategy by using Juran's term, Vital Few, to indicate an organization's highest priority areas of opportunity.

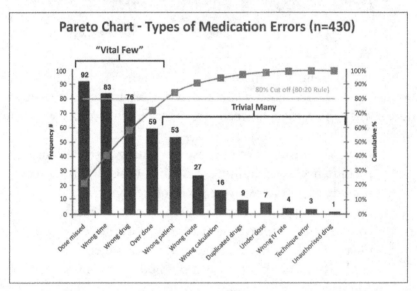

Pareto Chart Example

Juran is also credited with highlighting the role of culture on the quality levels in an organization. As you read this book further, you will see that the system is built to help address, understand, and continually improve your organization's culture.

Systems Thinking

Deming was a systems thinker and the first to urge corporate leaders to understand the system they are in and contribute to its improvement. The corollary to this, as he pointed out, were organizations that optimized individual functions (e.g., finance/cost) at the expense of the whole (e.g., sales/revenue). Deming summarized his thinking and his system in fourteen points, which he referred to as "The System of Profound Knowledge." A bit esoteric for my taste and not as simple or lean as it could be but, nonetheless, a system backed by a rich set of best practices, approaches, and statistical tools. Moving to this thinking helped Toyota develop its world-renowned Toyota Production System (TPS), which inarguably has led to their global leadership position in the automotive industry.

"The First Step Is Transformation Of The Individual"

Finally, Deming also spoke and wrote about the need for transformation at the individual level and believed that the transformation was discontinuous—as if a light switch goes on and you move from optimizing your function to understanding and optimizing the system, and from managing results to focusing and improving the processes that lead to the results. I agree with Deming, that this transformation is discontinuous, as I've witnessed the same in countless leaders and myself.

> "The first step is transformation of the individual. This transformation is discontinuous. Once the individual understands the system of profound knowledge, he will apply its principles in every kind of relationship with other people. He will have a basis for judgment of his own decisions and for transformation of the organizations that he belongs to. The individual, once transformed, will:
>
> - set an example
> - be a good listener, but will not compromise
> - continually teach other people
> - help people to pull away from their current practices and beliefs."

W. Edwards Deming

Executives in today's complex business environment face hundreds of tasks that need to be done. Many leaders have seemingly endless project lists, with most at risk or behind schedule. The most challenging but most important questions to answer are: "Which initiatives should be prioritized first?" and "Do we really need to readjust all tasks, or can some slip at the benefit of ensuring the most impactful projects are accomplished?" The choice toward a Vital Few and away from the trivial many is difficult yet offers the best chance at meaningfully changing performance.

Simplicity

One of the most salient features of HPMS is its simplicity. This is by design. Dick Palermo, the originator of HPMS, found Deming's statistical approaches too complex for most managers to grasp and benefit from, and the Malcolm Baldrige National Quality Award framework, also based on Deming, overly complex. Nonetheless, Dick believed deeply in the underlying principles laid out by Deming and set out to leverage them in a simpler, more approachable system. HPMS was his attempt to incorporate the powerful, proven quality principles and practices into a system that everyone in an organization can understand and contribute to.

One of the most frustrating aspects of the human condition is the tendency for individuals to add rather than subtract, and to believe by doing this they are doing their job. Instead, they are adding to the growing complexity and bureaucracy that slows everyone down.

Albert Einstein changed physics through his ability to explain his thought experiments in ways that most could understand and, notably, through his ability to simplify complex equations. He did not conceive, de novo, the relationship between energy(E), mass(m) and the speed of light(c); rather he simplified Hendrik Lorentz's 30 pages of formulae into these three terms and an exponent. This was his true genius. Managers and leaders who constantly seek to simplify their strategy, plans, processes, products and communications represent a similar sort of genius.

E=energy, m=mass and c=speed of light

I like to joke that Einstein would have made a terrific system thinker and quality-minded leader if he'd chosen that direction. Great minds can take complex businesses and processes and simplify them for improved speed, efficiency, and results.

Continuous Improvement

As the name implies, improvement of products, services, plans, and processes should be considered an ongoing, never-ending, closed-loop process. When adopted in conjunction with Pareto analysis, it allows the team or individual to focus on and achieve targeted breakthroughs. Once these have been accomplished, the team can then go back and refresh the gap and select the next Key Drivers of improvement.

Within a continuous improvement system or process, Pareto analysis provides a manager confidence to "not let perfection get in the way of good enough" as the next most important drivers will be picked up in the subsequent cycle. Deming's PDCA is a good example of a continuous improvement process applied to problem-solving:

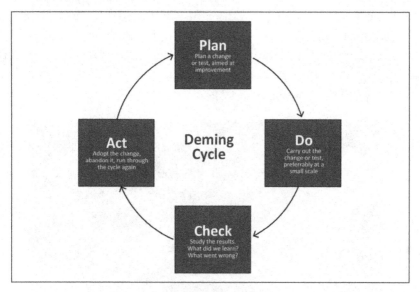

Deming's PDCA Cycle

These quality tools and methods, however, are useless absent a culture of continuous improvement. In successful quality cultures, ideas and inputs come from everywhere and most importantly from those closest to the activity. The management system and tools are engineered and supported to rapidly metabolize these inputs into improved processes, policies, products, and services. The Toyota Production System (TPS), more recently branded as "Lean manufacturing," represents a powerful example of such a system. Employees in quality cultures are encouraged to view everything through an improvement lens.

Benchmarking

I like to emphasize that benchmarking should always start with a result, preferably a "best" in class output, though in some cases, it can also be helpful to look at poor results and likewise learn from them. Dick Palermo emphasized the former with these words:

> "Seek and find best [process(es)] and steal shamelessly."
>
> —Dick Palermo

Taking this concept further, benchmarking best process(es) based on results should be a staple in your quality armamentarium. Let's say you would like to improve customer satisfaction with your products and services. You might start with the Ritz-Carlton based on their year-over-year-over-year best-in-class customer satisfaction results in J.D. Power, Condé Nast, AAA Four and Five Diamond Award, Forbes Travel Guide, *Travel + Leisure*, U.S. News & World Report, and many others. If you succeed in your effort and are able to go deep enough, you will find the process through which they consistently achieve these results.

Collaborative customer-facing process including clear escalation step...

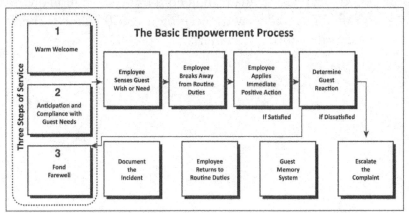

Example of Process Map for Customer Engagement at Ritz-Carlton
(source: Ritz-Carlton 1999 Malcolm Baldrige National Quality Award Application)

If interested in testing the quality of training and process focus at a Ritz, show this map and ask any employee to take you through it.

I will refer to this process as a benchmark in the IntraLase Rapid Adoption example in Chapter 8, The 4-Step Breakthrough Process™.

A final note on benchmarking: Best results are often associated with an organization in a specific period of time, under a specific CEO and team. They don't tend to last forever. For example:

- Xerox under David Kearns (1982–1990)
- GE under Jack Welch (1981– 001)
- FORD under Alan Mulally (2006–2014)
- Amazon under Jeff Bezos (1994–2021)
- Summit, IntraLase, ev3, and Wright Medical under Bob Palmisano (1997–2020)

These CEOs provide benchmarking opportunities within these time frames. Kearns and Palermo led the quality transformation at Xerox, which protected their domestic market share from Japanese competition and created share gains in Japan. Jack Welch created $400 billion in shareholder value, more than any peer CEO in that time period. And Alan Mulally took Ford from a $6 billion quarterly loss to profitability and growth resulting in a $50 billion increase in shareholder value during his tenure.

CHAPTER 4

PRINCIPLE 2: BUILDING A COALITION

The Importance Of People

Before we go deeper into the management system and its associated processes, I would like to highlight the importance of people. As success is limited absent the right people, your journey must start here.

Jim Collins and his team of twenty-one research associates at Stanford University School of Business understood the power of benchmarking explicitly in the research conducted to support publication of *Good to Great: Why Some Companies Make the Leap and Others Don't*. They started by looking at the financial performance of 1,435 companies over a forty-year period.

Their research identified eleven breakout companies that beat the general stock market by an average of seven times over a fifteen-year period. From this, they derived seven characteristics that described the best companies starting with **"Level V Leadership"** as described by humility and a deep, burning will to win. This contradicted the belief that the CEO should be a charismatic "rock star" and cheerleader. It also conformed to what I had experienced personally under Bill Freeman at Mentor and Bob Palmisano at Summit.

"First Who, Then What" represents the second of the seven characteristics derived by Collins and this team. Jim used a bus metaphor noting that great companies start by getting the right people on the bus, the wrong people off the bus, and the right people in the right seats. Great companies stick to this discipline: *first the people, then the direction.* This is precisely what Bob Palmisano did as Summit's CEO in a matter of months. If you have the wrong people on the bus, nothing else matters.

Moving to a more contemporary benchmark, based on financial results, is Amazon where CEO Jeff Bezos believes that people are his **"single most important factor for success"** and that **"nothing is more important"** than people. This is evidenced in a rigorous hiring process and a continually improving talent pool.

Creating A HPMS-Powered Movement

I have devoted an entire chapter to a simple but incredibly important concept: developing your initial following. Organizational adoption and movements do not occur all at once. Here is an example of how organizational transitions are perceived by most employees when announced versus what actually happens.

Perception:

The CEO announces the new management system to the organization with energy and excitement. The next day, 100% of employees are building their Success Trees, trying out the new tools, and speaking the language. Success!

Reality:

The CEO announces the new management system to the organization with energy and excitement.

- 10% of employees "get it" and are excited that the organization is using a system. They begin to use it.
- 80% of the organization thinks "that's nice" and goes on with their day.
- 10% of employees gossip about and undermine the management system.

True adoption of a system is a slog that requires you to win the hearts and minds of your employees, person-by-person. With this challenge in mind, a leader must be purposeful about their approach. The best place to start is with your leadership team.

To establish a continuous improvement culture and to drive HPMS adoption in particular, the number two (and three, four, etc.) are often more important than the CEO. The script goes like this: 1) the CEO announces that the company is going to adopt a new management system; 2) their number two leans in 110% and strives to push the system, its processes, and cultural elements even higher. In cases like this, HPMS adoption and business success are nearly ensured. The inverse is also true: when the number two doesn't embrace the system, the results are disastrous. Tony Hsieh made the point that the wrong executive hire costs Zappos $100 million, and I could not agree more.

Nourishing your first few followers as part of the process to build the organization's management system creates buy-in and gives you more sets of eyes to ensure the transition succeeds. It's no longer the CEO's flavor of the month; it is the leadership team's program.

Here are tips to consider when rolling the system out:

1. Ask for volunteers or assign direct responsibility for system elements to your leadership team around the cascade process, stoplight reporting, and breakthrough tickets.
2. Ensure that your Vital Few have executive sponsors. They will be accountable for the success of the organization's top initiatives.
3. Have your first few followers train the organization to the system. This will require them to hold a deeper level of knowledge about the system.
4. Be clear about having your executives use the system in their function—stoplight reports and breakthrough tickets. Employees will see their leader is role modeling the behaviors.
5. Reward and recognize leaders that adopt the system. Others should see that if they want to do well in the company, they need to operate utilizing the system.
6. Bring them to proficiency or help them out the door. It is common to have leaders that don't fully embrace your company's system. There should be no room in your leadership team for someone to do something else.

7. Similar to the point above, no one can be seen as above the system. Reed Hastings of Netflix had a saying that he didn't hire "brilliant jerks." Even if someone was talented, he saw the damage from people who operated outside the company's values. You cannot accept behavior that goes outside the system—others notice!

Once you create your first round of followers, you'll see the system take off. No longer do you need to stress about inspecting every aspect of your production or system processing; your leaders will help you there. The next task is to win the hearts and minds of your mid-tier management team (if your organization is large enough). This step usually takes more time but can be accelerated by considering the following:

1. Promotions should be weighted heavily to those who have succeeded in driving the system with their team. A senior leader in the program should exemplify the qualities of the system. Other employees will quickly take notice.
2. Communicate frequently with your teams about the value created through living the cultural elements and achieving milestones related to the Vital Few.
3. Invite mid-level leaders to your strategy workshops. Getting their fingerprints on the program will create buy-in.
4. Hold skip-level meetings to talk directly to next level leaders. You will get a good sense for how well the program is being adopted, and they will see you find the program important enough to discuss.
5. Whenever you are speaking to mid-level leaders, ask them to walk you through their Success Tree.

Please remember this simple formula: Great People + Great Management System = Great Results. Finally, you have the courage to change your management team sooner than later if it's not world-class.

The Significance of the First Follower

As mentioned, I've seen a lot of movies. From these experiences, and further supported by external benchmarks, clear patterns and truths are evident. One of the clearest is the need to create a movement toward a common goal. Regardless of how visionary and charismatic an organization's leader or CEO is, they cannot create a movement absent a first follower.

If you haven't seen Derek Sivers' TED Talk on this subject, I strongly encourage you to do so. https://www.ted.com/talks/derek_sivers_how_to_start_a_movement

In this entertaining three-minute video, you will witness and learn the fundamentals needed to start a movement. He draws a parallel of a guy dancing at an outdoor concert to the elements valuable in creating a movement in business. It sounds strange, but it is a fantastic illustration. Here are the main points he covers:

The leader (CEO) has the guts to stand out and be ridiculed. The leader's dance or process is simple and easy to follow. The leader embraces his first follower as an equal, clearly communicating the movement is not about himself.

The first follower transforms a "lone nut" into a leader.

New followers emulate the followers–not the leader. The movement is public and visible to all.

In two of our strongest engagements, ev3, Inc. and Spectranetics Corp., both of which sold for over $2 billion, we were honored to witness the creation of a movement along the same lines that Derek uses in his talk.

At ev3, CEO Bob Palmisano identified Stacy Enxing Seng, the Company's President, as a highly respected leader in the organization within his first few days at the company and knew that for him to be successful with his HPMS-powered movement, he would need more than her full support— and boy did he get it! Stacy embraced all HPMS elements with gusto and enthusiasm. She was especially great at sharing her Success Tree internally and externally. It was truly as if Bob said, "Stacy, let's fully commit to HPMS" and Stacy responded, "Okay, I will do it 110%." With that, their movement was underway.

With a great deal of success in her career and education prior to meeting Bob and HPMS, she easily could have said a number of things that we often hear such as "This is too simple," "We are different," "The Tree and icons seem "hokey" and we have twenty priorities; how can we possibly be successful with just five?"—all of which present, in our opinion, as classic change resistance.

Not only did Stacy support Bob, she became an immense force for HPMS and used her Success Tree everywhere she went. She energized her leaders to follow her lead, and over time, people wanted to join in because it looked amazing from the outside. Without Stacy, Bob would have been a lone dancer and had difficulty getting the system out of the boardroom.

Whether it is attracting people to join you to dance with them at an outdoor concert or building a coalition in business, the importance of nurturing followers cannot be ignored. Leaders shouldn't just assume people will follow them because of their title or personality. By standing out with a simple process and finding a strong number two, you have a much greater chance of creating a movement.

CHAPTER 5

PRINCIPLE 3: AFFIRMING YOUR DIRECTION AND CULTURE

Once we have the right people committed to building a great company, it's time to define where we want to go and how we must behave to get there. When done correctly, you'll ignite the passion and discretionary effort in your team and reach heights that many would think impossible. When done incorrectly, you'll likely demotivate people who will give minimal effort to make it through the day and achieve average to below-average results.

Virtually everyone has been on a great team sometime in their lives, whether in sports, work, or even board games. Through decades of research, the best teams and companies have these elements:

1. A prescriptive Vision: A clear view of where the team will be in the future. By creating an image of how you will be perceived by the world, the odds of reaching it increase substantially.

2. A set of Shared Values: Behaviors that define how a team will work together. If done correctly, these will unlock the talent and energy of the team to efficiently and effectively achieve their Vision.

3. A directive Mission statement: A present-tense statement describing what the team does to achieve the Vision, how it does it, for whom, and sometimes why.

Each element is powerful, and you don't have to do them all well, but it helps. Netflix, with an amazing growth curve in the early 2000s, focused mostly on Values, while Medtronic, the largest and most successful medical device maker, has traditionally focused more on their Mission. The goal should be to clearly define each and work on the areas that will make the most impact to you and your company.

Creating a Prescriptive Vision

This is likely a chapter that many have been waiting for as it transitions from the foundational HPMS elements to building a system for your company.

The first step in developing your Vision statement is to be prescriptive in measurable terms. For example, what will our revenues and gross margins look like? What markets will we develop and what share should we own? These measures will serve as a reference point. From there it's about going beyond these measures and using your imagination, which is unlimited!

"Imagination is more important than knowledge. For knowledge is limited to all we now know and understand, while imagination embraces the entire world, and all there ever will be to know and understand."

—Albert Einstein

Einstein changed physics largely through the use of his imagination, not bound by what was known at the time. This is not easy to do for most traditional managers, but to the extent possible, please take on this mindset.

Over the years we have benchmarked best Vision statements, based on results, and have found them to possess these qualities:

1. They represent a visible future state, often written in future tense.
2. They represent bold claims which, over time, the organization can defend and ultimately own.
3. They are audacious and sometimes written by organizations who have no present right to the claim.
4. They are concise, memorable, and motivational.
5. They guide decisions and actions.

Here are a few examples of best Vision statements based on results. Note how each makes a **bold**, aspirational claim:

A. Microsoft's early Vision statement:

"Early on, Paul Allen and I set the goal of a computer on every desk and in every home. It was a bold idea and a lot of people thought we were out of our minds to imagine it was possible."

—Bill Gates

B. Amazon's current Vision statement:

"To be the Earth's most customer-centric company, where customers can find and discover anything they might want to buy online."

C. The Moon landing of July 20, 1969:

Kennedy stood before Congress on May 25, 1961 and proposed that the US:

"...should commit itself to achieving the goal, before this decade is out, of landing a man on the Moon and returning him safely to Earth."

—John Fitzgerald Kennedy

D. Alan Mulally's "ONE FORD"

ONE FORD

ONE TEAM • ONE PLAN • ONE GOAL

ONE TEAM

People working together as a lean, global enterprise for automotive leadership, as measured by:

Customer, Employee, Dealer, Investor, Supplier, Union/Council, and Community Satisfaction

ONE PLAN

- Aggressively restructure to operate profitably at the current demand and changing model mix.
- Accelerate development of new products our customers want and value.
- Finance our plan and improve our balance sheet.
- Work together effectively as one team.

ONE GOAL

An exciting viable Ford delivering profitable growth for all

By now, you should have the sense that no two Vision statements are alike, that there's no formula from which it can be derived and, perhaps, that it's a bit of an artform. You should also know that they can change over time. Once Microsoft accomplished its original Vision of a computer on every desk and in every home, they evolved to their current Vision statement, which is:

"To help people and businesses throughout the world realize their full potential."

Vision statements are first and foremost meant to inspire and mobilize your employees. The best statements inspire customers and shareholders as well, but this is not a requirement.

The Transformative Power of "Wicked" Strategic Clarity

Spectranetics®

Spectranetics Corp. was founded by Robert Glolobic, PhD, and Johan Sverdrup in 1984 with a vision to leverage excimer laser technology to treat coronary lesions and restore blood flow to affected areas. With limited funding and a great deal of persistence, they received FDA approval for treatment of peripheral and coronary arterial disease in 1993.

The next fifteen years, however, would prove challenging as the company survived the death of both founders, a bitter class-action lawsuit, and a federal investigation that threatened the firm's existence. While the promise of the technology was enormous, revenue growth was an ongoing concern for the company.

In 2011, Board Chair John Fletcher hired Scott Drake as CEO to take Spectranetics to new levels of performance. Scott and his COO Shar Matin believed in the importance of operating through a proven management system and processes based on quality principles.

After evaluating a number of potential systems, they selected the High Performance Management System (HPMS) based on its past performance in the med-tech sector. They were further drawn to HPMS based on its ability to provide "wicked" strategic clarity along with a healthy balance on culture and teammate engagement.

"Mission 300"

Shortly after selecting the management system, Scott took his leadership team offsite to take the first steps toward building and implementing his management system. They started the workshop with a "Prescription Vision" exercise, where they were asked to articulate their "Desired State" for Spectranetics in five years in broad strategic terms and, where possible, in objective measures.

Driven by Scott's passion to double the size of the business to $300 million, an energetic and engaged discussion ensued. The team was further guided and advised to develop a concise and memorable statement that embodied Scott's prescriptive revenue target. With all of the above factored in, the team reached consensus on "Mission 300" as their key goal and "rallying cry." From that point forward, everything in the company would have to align with this concise, memorable, aspirational, and visible future state.

"That first HPMS offsite meeting was seminal in that it aligned us as a team on peripheral expansion and lead management as our Vital Few. Prior to that, we were in coronary, peripheral, and lead management—with a constant pull and push where to invest. As "Mission 300" took hold, it became clear that we could not get there in a reasonable period of time with the resources we had by focusing on all three."

—Shar Matin, COO

Scott and Shar also embraced the system's structured problem-solving Breakthrough Process to solve key problems and discover opportunities. The process focused on creating empowered teams to solve problems with facts and data rather than through political maneuverings. This became clear to the employees when, in some cases, Scott and Shar demanded they see a Pareto chart before making any further decisions. Over time, this became a common language within Spectranetics, allowing faster, higher quality decisions, and sustainable solutions.

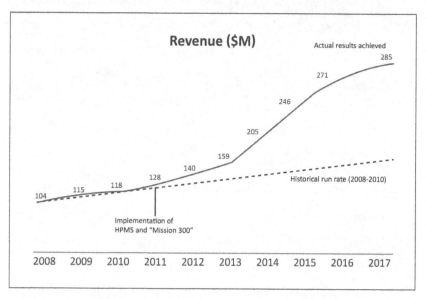

Spectranetics Revenue 2008 - 2017

"Mission 300"

Scott's team at Spectranetics embraced all elements of the High Performance Management system to align his people, culture, and resources and achieve $285 million in revenue and a $2.2 billion sale to Royal Phillips in 2017—a result that may not have been achieved absent the disciplined, data-driven system and processes they embraced.

"HPMS has been a cornerstone of our success and value creation over the past five plus years. Along with talent management, execution rigor, and our focus on culture, HPMS has ensured that we drive the 'Vital Few' initiatives that matter most to teammates and customers."

—Scott Drake, CEO Spectranetics (2016)

After you have created a Vision statement for your organization, put it into action immediately. Many people have worked at companies with ineffective Vision statements, so they will naturally go about their day and see them as words on a page. Here are a few ways to bring your Vision to life:

1. Make it tangible and show progression: If we compare our progress toward our Vision to a group of mountain climbers making their way to the top of Everest, as the leader, we will want to show the team how far along we are toward the summit at regular intervals. Though many Vision statements are intangible, it can still be beneficial to demonstrate progress. If you'd like to take a more quantitative approach, you can test agreement with your statement via key stakeholders. Accept low agreement early on with increasing levels of agreement as you progress to your destination.

2. When making decisions, go out of your way to tie the decision to the Vision: Much like any new habit, you need

to first be purposeful in using it to create a habit. The more individuals do this, the more likely you will succeed. Note that this comes with risks. If you push too hard, people will see it as window dressing and contrived.

3. Share your view of why you are excited about the Vision and ask others about it. When you talk to employees, ask them what they think will be different when we achieve the Vision and how great it will be when we arrive there.

Driving Performance Through Shared Values

Proper development and authentic adoption of Shared Values may be the most powerful single element in your company's HPMS. Work is more efficient and effective when individual and team behaviors are consistent and predictable, resulting in higher quality levels and lower costs.

Shared Values, especially when embedded in your performance management process, simplify reward/recognition and dismissal decisions. They should serve as a foundational element in your hiring practice. They should also drive higher levels of employee engagement and customer satisfaction. Shared Values are not a soft or "feel good" element; when properly developed and authentically adopted, they are a competitive advantage.

Shared Values improve hand-offs and teamwork

To the average leader, values may feel mushy and intangible. Most of us have been on a high-performing team at one point in our career. Was there something significantly different about how the people behaved on that team compared to those on the worst-performing from your experience? What made it different? Did the team members hold each other accountable? Was there open and honest communication? Did you just have the right environment for talented people to want to join? Whatever the case is, it often comes down to the values and behaviors within the group.

By not defining and driving a set of Shared Values, an organization will naturally create their own unsaid rules. The reason we create these and spend time to define them is to help steer the organization to a place that best suits the needed performance of the organization.

How many Values should an organization have? This is a common question and area of debate for many of our clients. In the eighties and nineties, having eight was common. Ritz-Carlton defined theirs in 1999 and they have twelve. We recommend a shorter list of four to six.

Why is having too many a problem? Our brains can only take so much. It's hard enough to change our routines; imagine trying to get one thousand or ten thousand people to do so. By focusing on the message, you have a greater chance of success. Ritz-Carlton reviews one value a day and with twelve, they only cover each value twice a month. If they had only four, they would discuss it five times a month! I am not saying that Ritz doesn't have a great system, but most companies today don't have the infrastructure in place to train and enforce twelve values.

I also bet that you have worked at a few companies that had a set of Values. Can you remember them all? Do you think all employees could?

So how many? As the world becomes more complicated, we recommend an organization take the crawl, walk, run, approach, and select four to six as a starting point. Since HPMS has a regular feedback loop (usually every six months), you can always improve them later if necessary. If you are struggling with four, DON'T ADD MORE! Find out what is getting in your way and focus on a deeper behavior change rather than more words on a page.

We further recommend you develop your company's Shared Values through a highly inclusive workshop leveraging a structured problem-solving process along these lines:

1. Brainstorm the Current State of the culture and behaviors (good and bad)?

2. Brainstorm the Desired State of the culture and behaviors?
3. Vote and reach consensus on the Shared Values that, when adopted authentically, will close the identified cultural gap.

This exercise can be done by an employee survey or in a workshop or series of workshops. Typically, it will generate a list of twenty to forty Values for consideration. Your next step should be to identify the top 20% (typically four to eight) most transformational Values through employee votes.

Once you arrive at your agreed Shared Values, you or a small team should write short, one-sentence definitions for each and ensure the Values and these definitions are visibly displayed in all key areas of work.

Your Shared Values should also be incorporated into your management system by displaying them on each Success Tree and, ideally, by incorporating them into your performance management process. On this score, each should allow for a one to five performance range supported by examples. We recommend you avoid values like integrity in your system as it's binomial: an employee demonstrates it every day or they don't; if the latter, it should be cause for dismissal.

Leading Change when Business is Good --
IBM Shared Values

As IBM's CEO, Sam Palmisano knew he couldn't directly develop, manufacture or market their products and services. He knew he couldn't balance the books, build financial models, maintain their facilities, or sell, ship or receive product. He did know, however, that he could shape the culture, and he saw that as his highest priority. In 2003, Sam set out to improve the company's culture through a refreshed set of Shared

Values. His first step was to engage ≅50,000 employees in a three-day "ValuesJam" on their intranet. Sam and a group of 300 executives reviewed the employee feedback and reached consensus on the following three Values:

1. Dedication to every client's success
2. Innovation that matters—for our company and the world
3. Trust and personal responsibility in all relationships

"Values, for us, aren't soft. They're the basis of what we do, our mission as a company. They're a touchstone for decentralized decision-making. It used to be a rule of thumb that 'people don't do what you expect; they do what you inspect.' My point is that it's just not possible to inspect everyone anymore. But you also can't just let go of the reins and let people do what they want without guidance or context. You've got to create a management system that empowers people and provides a basis for decision-making that is consistent with who we are at IBM."

— Sam Palmisano, CEO

Constructing A Directive Mission Statement

There is a reasonable amount of confusion between Vision statements and Mission statements and rightfully so as some organizations combine the two into one statement—generally a Mission statement includes a bold claim (see Tesla example at end of this chapter). That said, the following table provides a helpful summary comparison:

Mission vs. Vision

"Route"	"Destination"
• Concise [present tense] statement describing what we do for whom • Can include how and why we do it • Internally focused • Clearly informs all stakeholders, especially employees, of the organization's core purpose	• Concise [future tense] • Aspirational • Memorable • Guides decisions and actions • External, market-oriented • Expresses how the organization wants to be perceived by the world in the future

A well-constructed directive Mission statement provides direction and "constancy of purpose." Written in present tense, it should answer at least three of the following four questions:

1. What do we do?
2. For whom do we do it?
3. How do we do it?
4. Why do we do it?

Your Mission statement should be constructed in a concise, memorable sentence or two that answers most of these questions for key stakeholders. It is especially useful for new employees or partners. When done well, it should also help your organization stay focused and "stick to your knitting."

When Individuals Are in a Crisis:
a Mission Statement in Action

When individuals are in a crisis, we sometimes forget what we are there for, and a strong Mission statement can help remind us all what we stand for and allow us to drive higher quality decisions and actions.

This is the Mission statement we initially developed at IntraLase Corp. A bit wordy but nonetheless answers the four questions and most definitely provided clear direction for the organization.

We present proprietary femtosecond laser technology and provide the leading all-laser alternative to the mechanical microkeratome. (what)

We provide world-class training to surgeons and maintain excellent relationships with our customers [doctors, providers, and distributors]. (how and for whom)

We do this to enable patients to choose vision correction surgery with confidence and to provide appropriate financial performance for shareholders and customers. (why)

Visually managed through visible Success Trees, training and communication, most employees could recite its key points. After we'd hit our inflection point at IntraLase Corp. and were growing rapidly in the US, Western Europe, and key Asia markets, we started doing business in the Middle East and were soon faced with some unique support challenges. With the 2006 Lebanon War (also called the 2006 Israel-Hezbollah War) underway, the region was in a state of unrest and few employees outside of sales were interested in traveling there.

I recall a specific challenge to our Mission at this time, and this is how it played out: We had successfully sold and installed a laser in one of these newly targeted markets. Unfortunately, we could not find a volunteer from our Clinical Applications team to go there and train the surgeon and his staff. We called a meeting and started discussion options, including sending one of our US surgeon customers there to execute the training. We were feeling okay about that approach and thought it might work...until a junior team member stepped up and said, "Our Mission says that we provide world-class training, and this doesn't feel world-class. "With that comment, we snapped back into "our knitting" and came up with a direct, world-class solution that delighted the customer and ensured successful procedure adoption.

Amazon Mission And Vision

Mission statements differ significantly from future-tense prescriptive Vision statements. Let's examine the difference between Amazon's Mission and Vision statements as a benchmark:

Amazon's Vision: **"To be the Earth's most customer-centric company, where customers can find and discover anything they might want to buy online."**

Broken down: **"To be** (in the future) **the Earth's most** (superlative) **customer-centric company, where customers can find and discover anything they might want to buy online."**

Amazon's Mission: **"We strive to offer our customers the lowest possible prices, the best available selection, and the utmost convenience."**

Broken down: **"We strive** (present tense) **to offer our customers** (for whom) **the lowest possible prices, the best available selection, and the utmost convenience."** (what we do)

The answer to "why" is obvious: To provide a reasonable return to our shareholders, as such it's omitted from the statement. I find this true in most for-profit entities.

Medtronic Mission Statement

Sometimes, generally in larger organizations, the Mission statement serves as the foundational element for the corporation providing a common purpose across multiple strategic business units. Medtronic's Mission, **"To contribute to human welfare by application of biomedical engineering in the research, design, manufacture, and sale of instruments or appliances that alleviate pain, restore health, and extend life,"** provides a powerful and effective example of this approach.

Medtronic's Mission, **"To contribute to human welfare by application of biomedical engineering in the research, design, manufacture, and sale of instruments or appliances that alleviate pain, restore health, and extend life"**

Medtronic Mission Medallion

Medtronic visually manages their Mission through the Medtronic Mission medallion, ensuring that nearly all employees worldwide can recite it. Medtronic introduced a Mission and Medallion ceremony in 1974 to celebrate its fifteenth anniversary. Now held many times a year at facilities all over the world, the ceremony is a symbolic way to bring new employees together behind a common purpose. Each employee receives a medallion as a reminder of the honor and responsibility they have in fulfilling the Mission.

Tesla: a Hybrid Mission-Vision Statement

Some companies prefer a single hybrid Mission-Vision statement by combining a bold claim with answers to "what, for whom, how, and why." I find this perfectly acceptable and offer Tesla's Vision statement as an example.

> "To create the most compelling car company of the 21st century by driving the world's transition to electric vehicles."

Let's break it down:

> "To create the most compelling car company of the 21st century (bold claim in future tense) by driving the world's transition to electric vehicles." (what and how)

I'd like to close this chapter by pointing out that there's no absolute correct way to write your Vision and Mission statements. You can go further yourself by looking at the "best" companies and how they approach these critical items.

CHAPTER 6

PRINCIPLE 4: LISTENING TO YOUR KEY STAKEHOLDERS

Stakeholder inputs could have been included in chapter five as a fundamental quality practice; however, it flows better here as it is critical to building a great Success Tree™, which is covered in the next chapter. The quality of your management system's output is directly proportional to the quality of the system's inputs; as such, I can't overstate the importance of properly collecting, analyzing, prioritizing, and acting on these inputs in your system. This is exhibited by almost any feedback loop:

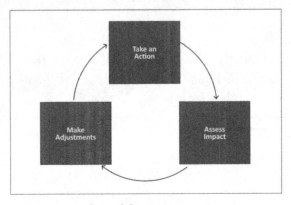

Closed-loop Process

If you receive no, or even false, signals after taking an action, you are unlikely to continuously improve. Therefore, it is vitally important that we have access to the impacted parties to assess their needs as time progresses. This applies to nearly everything in life—automobiles continually assess the fuel/air mixture and make changes in milliseconds; when you ride your bike, your brain makes calculations based on your body weight, movement, and line of sight.

Let's start by identifying the common stakeholder groups. In virtually all organizations, they can be organized into these three groups:

1. Customers
2. Employees
3. Shareholders/Financial Community

Depending on the nature and scope of your business, there may be a few more to consider. Note that in Alan Mulally's "ONE FORD," one-page strategic plan, he included, "ONE TEAM: People working together as a lean, global enterprise for automotive leadership, as measured by *Customer, Employee, Dealer, Investor, Supplier, Union/Council, and Community Satisfaction.*" So, as Alan built his system, he incorporated seven inputs—the three above, plus:

1. Dealer
2. Supplier
3. Union/Council
4. Community

I think you get the idea. If you are running a large, global enterprise such as Ford, you will likely want to go beyond the top three. For simplicity's sake, the remainder of this text will focus on customer, employee, and shareholder inputs.

Voice Of The Customer

Customers are the lifeblood of any organization. While this is obvious, when we get into our day-to-day job, we sometimes forget what it is like to be a customer ourselves. We've all had an experience with a product or service we told our friends about. It is highly likely that your recommendation led others to purchase that product or service. The opposite has likely been true too, where you were disappointed with a product and told others to steer clear.

A customer's willingness to recommend your company is one of the most important leading indicators you can measure within your company. While most companies spend enormous amounts of time understanding prior purchasing behaviors, they often leave out important questions such as: were they satisfied with the product or service, and will they buy your product again and recommend it to qualified others in the future?

The impacts of having delighted customers are enormous, including brand loyalty, a base that will market your product on your behalf and, of course, ongoing revenues.

You'd be surprised to learn that many companies don't have their primary customers defined. This is always a good first step. Every company has myriad stakeholders—medical device companies have the FDA, distributors, nurses, doctors, administration, community, patients, and several other groups that have requirements, but not all are the primary decision-makers. Defining and prioritizing your primary decision-maker and ensuring they are delighted is a huge step forward. It follows the adage, if everyone is a priority, no one is a priority, and everyone will receive an equal and numb experience with the company. Yes, we want everyone to enjoy working with us, but it is nearly impossible to make everyone happy!

We recommend that companies regularly collect their customers' voice and utilize it in their strategy planning process. By bringing the customer into the room, we can ensure that we are living in reality rather than an insulated bubble. We have seen leadership meetings where everyone says things are going well, then hear a different reality from the customers. Perhaps the company will continue to get lucky and grow, but at some point, ignoring your customers' needs is unsustainable.

We typically like to understand the customer experience in Ritz-Carlton's terms, "from the warm greeting to the fond farewell." By measuring, analyzing, and acting on the opportunities, we can build an enduring customer base.

IntraLase Corp. and the Relentless Pursuit of Customer Satisfaction

This is a story highlighting our Voice of Customer (VOC) process, a foundational element of our high-performance management system (HPMS) and the key impact it had on decision-making and our ultimate success in the marketplace.

Through this process, we regularly measured customer satisfaction with their journey from "the greeting to the farewell" as well as overall willingness to recommend our company to a colleague. We understood their journey started with sales and continued through installation, training, and support. Additionally, we understood that product performance was critical to satisfaction so likewise, we tested satisfaction with key elements such as ease-of-use, reliability, speed, and clinical outcomes. We also put ourselves up for measurement and included a statement regarding the quality of leadership.

We also asked the following open-ended question: "If IntraLase could improve one or two important things, what would you recommend?" In this sense, we are asking the customer to help us Pareto their needs. In the analysis step, we measure satisfaction scores as well as correlations to overall satisfaction. Correlation is absolutely critical to identifying the "right things" as score alone can be misleading. We also performed comment analysis as a key analysis step.

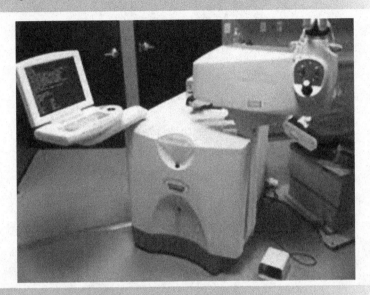

IntraLase FS Femtosecond Laser

The first generation IntraLase laser, launched in 2002, operated at 10 kHz and, depending on your preferred spot/line separation, could take up to two minutes to complete a corneal dissection or LASIK "flap." This compared unfavorably with the ≅10 seconds it took with a traditional microkeratome. Through our voice of customer process, we understood this to be the number one opportunity for improvement. In response, we launched the second generation in 2004 at 15 kHz enabling procedure times of ≅1 minute, and the third generation in 2005 at 30 kHz and ≅30-second procedure times.

At IntraLase, we refreshed the strategy or Vital Few priorities on a six-month cycle. Voice of the customer, employee and shareholder are all critical inputs to these sessions, and, as we like to say, the quality of the output is dependent on the quality of the input.

As we prepared for our early 2005 strategy session, or HPMS Offsite, our customer data and this analysis pointed to an inconvenient truth: the speed of the system remained the lowest score/highest correlation to satisfaction item—trumping, once again, improvements in ease-of- use, reliability, and consumables. The survey results, at first, were not well received, creating a sense of discomfort and tension among the leadership team, particularly in R&D. The existing assumption was that we'd solved for speed and that we could go on to the next series of product improvements.

After a great deal of discussion about market segmentation, resources, and feasibility, however, we reached consensus on a plan to double the speed of the laser—to 60 kHz—in less than one year.

Eleven months later, in early 2006, we launched the 60 kHz system touting $\cong$15 second procedures times. This breakthrough, which came at the expense of many other projects, allowed us to penetrate the high-volume surgeon segment and continue our march to become the standard-of-care. I can still recall specific surgeons who switched from the blade to the laser on the release of the 60 kHz system.

While an obvious concept, we find that many businesses struggle to truly listen and respond to their customers. Many focus solely on the financial drivers, pushing for more systems in the market by competing on price or features, rather than finding what the customer wants, improving it, and building loyalists who will market your product for you.

Voice of the Employee

Bringing the employee voice into the room is equally as important as bringing your customer voice into the room. If you believe that employees want to do what is best for your customers and shareholders, we should take their input regarding how we can improve as they are often more intimate with what is going on in the company than you.

As with our customers, we want to understand the employee's willingness to recommend your company. We all have hard days and employees understand that work isn't a vacation, but people will still recommend a company to their friends or family members if they feel respected and that their role is meaningful.

By measuring their "willingness to recommend" and striving to continually improve it, you will build a loyal and productive employee base that is more likely to delight customers and drive financial results. If you don't focus on intently listening to your employees, they are more likely to leave or give the bare minimum.

**Eliminating Functional Silos through Data,
Analysis, and Action!**

RxSight® is a privately held corporation that recently commercialized the world's first and only intraocular lens (IOL) that can be customized after cataract surgery delivering superior visual outcomes.

When Andy Corley joined as Chairman in 2015, he successfully recruited industry all-stars Ron Kurtz, MD, and Eric Weinberg to run the company. With new capital and experienced management, the company relocated to Aliso Viejo, CA. and grew rapidly from 2015 to 2017. The rapid growth, however, did not come without opportunities in employee engagement.

As experienced and successful HPMS practitioners, Kurtz and Weinberg believed strongly in the need to measure and continually improve their employees' willingness to recommend RxSight as a place of work. To help accomplish this, they retained Haffey&Co. to distribute and analyze an annual employee survey.

The November 2017 survey revealed a significant problem or opportunity for improvement in the area of cross-functional communication and cooperation. In fact, only 39% of employees felt it was satisfactory, making it the lowest score item on the survey. While still a young company with less than 100 employees, functional silos were going up in critical areas of the company (e.g., R&D and manufacturing). Finger-pointing was trumping collaboration, and if allowed to continue, the company would have been severely limited in its ability to execute on its vision.

As a result, Kurtz and Weinberg quickly updated their Success Tree indicating "Cross-functional communication and cooperation" as the new Employee Branch Vital Few initiative. A cross-functional, cross-layer team was formed and, with further support from Haffey&Co., went deep into the "Current State." Understanding that they couldn't solve the problem with a peanut butter approach, the team deployed a follow-on survey to discover the specific handoffs and relationships that were driving the low score from which the following Pareto chart was derived.

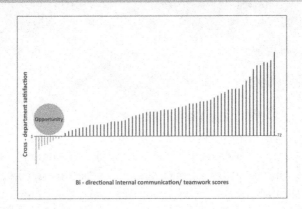

Pareto of Hand-offs

The team decided to focus on the seven relationships out of the total of seventy-two in the company for immediate improvement action. The affected groups were then gathered and went through rapid problem-solving exercises (e.g., Current State -> Desired State -> Recommended process and plan to implement) with respect to each of the seven areas of opportunity.

To follow up on the effectiveness of the changes and actions, RxSight deployed a follow-on survey in June 2018. The survey reflected a breakthrough in this metric—from 39% to 60% in six months. The company has continued to measure and improve this critical metric in each successive survey, showing that the breakthrough level of performance achieved is sustainable.

Through this focused effort, RxSight addressed a major issue which could have dragged down the company's performance. Instead, they leveraged the talents and passion of a diverse team, focused on root cause, and eliminated barriers to improve the way work gets done and achieve their vision.

Voice of the Shareholder

The third major input we strive to bring into the room is your company's shareholders and/or its financial stakeholders. We have found that actively interviewing the board of directors, key shareholders, and analysts is unique, and many thank us for taking a moment to speak to them directly to record and articulate their views. While we ask our customers and employees about their willingness to recommend, we usually work to understand shareholder's vision for the company three to five years from now in broad strategic terms and, where possible, in measurable objective terms.

This process does amazing things for leaders and managers who are rarely exposed to the shareholders by giving everyone a bigger picture regarding how their role impacts the future success of the company.

By collecting and sharing these stakeholder voices with our team, employees will no longer see themselves as here to make the CEO or manager happy but working as a team to build delighted customers, motivated employees, and satisfied shareholders.

Listening to Shareholders and Finding the Way to Profitability

Sometimes when interviewing a company's shareholder representatives, usually the BOD, strong themes emerge that cannot be ignored. In one client's case, it was clear that the board was seriously concerned with the corporation's path to profitability. The company was in growth mode, where it isn't abnormal to run a deficit, but this company's losses of $100 million per year on revenue under $1 billion was too much to handle given their business maturity.

The leadership team took the shareholder feedback and escalated it to a Vital Few with the intention of moving from $100 million annual losses to, at a minimum, breaking even. The CFO ecstatically volunteered to not only sponsor but lead the team. The team adopted the Breakthrough Process, which helps organize the project and improve effectiveness.

He collected a core team that ran across several functions with profit and loss responsibility as well as extended teams to do further digging. The core team could discuss the sensitive topics, such as head count and long-term strategies to deprioritize certain areas. In contrast, the extended teams were focused on finding opportunities within the realm of waste reduction and revenue upside. The groups looked everywhere, not just at the traditional cost-cutting targets.

Over thirty days, the teams sifted through the Current State, identified opportunities, and built a priority matrix that rated the projects based on risk, reward, and ease of implementation. Through the visualization shown below, seven projects stood out from the pack. Interestingly, the top two were unknown in the organization as significant levers for improvement—only through the investigation did we learn the power and significance of the opportunities.

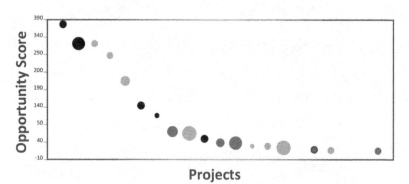

Projects

Projects higher up on the Y-axis are easier and faster to implement. The bubble size corresponds to the EBITA impact, and the shading of the bubble indicates execution risk, where darker shading indicates lower risk.

Over the next six months, the projects were tracked and executed in the weekly stoplight report. Through the team's effort and the more significant organizational push, the company was able to bring their earnings before interest and taxes (EBIT) under control. Minimal cuts were made, and the customers and employees felt minimal impact.

Nearly all companies are faced with some level of this opportunity at some point in their journey. Any leadership team can make across the board cuts, which can cause harm and unintended consequences. Making broad cuts also leads to poor behavior such as "If you don't use it, you lose it," where leaders play games and plan how to maintain their budgets year over year.

By listening and acting on stakeholder input and using the Breakthrough Process, the empowered team was able to take a broad look at how the company functioned and make tradeoffs that did not sacrifice the long-term success of the company. The team was given a goal and found a balance between top-line opportunities, waste reductions, and head-count reductions that best fit the overall company strategy. They did not let their functional or parochial interest get in the way. Additionally, the results continued through the training of these team members and driving a culture around continually improving EBIT and building a sustainable business.

CHAPTER 7

PRINCIPLE 5: DRIVING "WICKED" STRATEGIC CLARITY

Developing your Corporate Success Tree

Your top-level or "corporate" Success Tree represents the highest level strategy document in the organization. As strategy is essentially about making choices and not trying to be everything to everybody, the one-page approach helps facilitate decisions at this level. The Tree should be visible in key areas of work and clearly communicated and understood by all in the organization. As you cascade the corporate Tree through the organization, the goals and objectives will transition from strategic to tactical, yet all in the organization know the most important things or Vital Few initiatives that will drive success.

We utilize the Success Tree to accomplish focus and organize the elements of the management system. The Success Tree represents a one-page strategic plan for your organization as well as for all functions, departments, and individuals. Through the cascade process and by making each visible in its respective area of work, the Success Tree helps align your people, processes, and resources to your strategy.

In most organizations, there is a marked lack of alignment between functions, departments and individuals. Using a rowboat metaphor, folks rarely row together resulting in a great deal of waste and inefficiency. The following graphic resonates with most in these organizations:

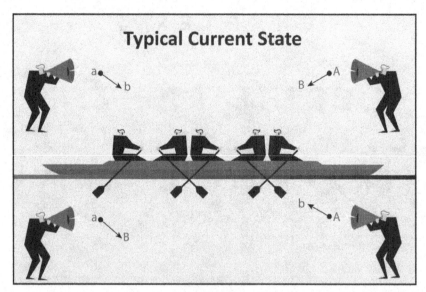

Lack of Alignment

Imagine that the four leaders depicted are functional leaders in sales, finance, operations and supply chain. Each is saying the organization needs to move from "A" or "a" to "B" or "b." Sadly, they do not work in a system where "A," the Current State and "B," the Desired State, are developed and agreed on by cross-functional, cross-layer teams. It's also unlikely that these goals are visible throughout the organization, otherwise it would be easy to call out the misalignment. You might say it's the epitome of an organization that optimizes functions at the expense of the whole.

Let's imagine a different organization working through their company's HPMS where cross-functional, cross-layer teams work through a common process, using common language to reach consensus on the Current State (where we are now) and the Desired State (where we need to go). This organization's rowboat would then look something like this:

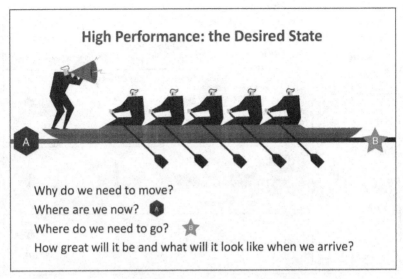

Alignment

A well-developed Success Tree generally includes these six elements:

1. A concise, aspirational, and motivational Vision statement that guides decisions and actions
2. A concise, memorable directive Mission statement that answers fundamental questions regarding what the organization does today, for whom, how and why
3. A short list of transformational Values that, when adopted in an authentic way, ensure behavior necessary to achieve your Vision
4. A customer branch indicating one or more Vital Few opportunities for improved customer satisfaction
5. An employee branch indicating one or more Vital Few opportunities for improved employee satisfaction
6. A shareholder or financial branch indicating one or more Vital Few opportunities for improved financial performance

And generally, it looks like this:

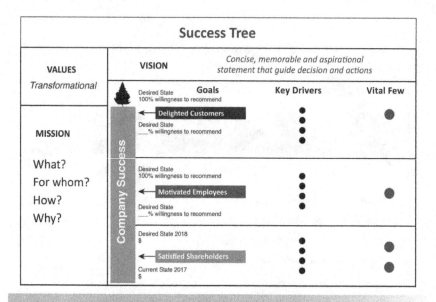

Success Tree				
VALUES *Transformational*	**VISION**	*Concise, memorable and aspirational statement that guide decision and actions*		
		Goals	**Key Drivers**	**Vital Few**
MISSION What? For whom? How? Why?	Company Success	Desired State 100% willingness to recommend ← Delighted Customers Desired State ___% willingness to recommend		
		Desired State 100% willingness to recommend ← Motivated Employees Desired State ___% willingness to recommend		
		Desired State 2018 $ ← Satisfied Shareholders Current State 2017 $		

The Power of a One-Page Strategic Plan—
at Summit Technology, Inc.

Your Success Tree, when properly constructed and managed, serves as your one-page strategic plan. The overarching theme for your Tree is simplicity. Through the one-page requirement, you and your organization are forced to make strategic choices.

I vividly recall my first experience with this powerful tool at Summit Technology, Inc. in 1997 and how it helped guide me, my organization, and our company. In the months prior to implementation, we had at least twenty strategic priorities and initiatives, many of which would change from day-to-day based on an event, anecdote, or executive hubris. One executive, who will remain anonymous, announced that the Tree was in fact too simple. In his words, "We have over twenty priorities as an organization. How are we supposed to reduce the list to five and be effective?" This executive was a complicator who enjoyed the swirl associated with our Current State and, coincidentally, was let go some time later.

In my case, it was liberating, representing a clear path out of the jungle, as I expressed to Dick Palermo about an hour into our first offsite session with him.

Prior to our application of this tool, Summit was in three distinct businesses: 1) excimer laser development, manufacturing, and marketing, 2) laser vision centers including doctors and staff, and 3) mail order contact lenses. Believing in the fundamentals of the laser business and market potential, the first big decision we made was to divest our vision centers and contact lens businesses and focus 100% of our resources on the core laser business. With these decisions, our transformation was underway.

With our heightened focus on the laser business, we further committed to the following Vital Few priorities:

> Meaning more to our customers and helping them grow their practices
>
> Increasing the range of FDA approvals on our laser
>
> Upgrading our talent and, in particular, senior management
>
> Implementing a new ERP system (Oracle)
>
> Selling more laser systems and procedures

These five were placed on the Success Tree framework and made visible throughout the organization. My Tree was placed on the wall in my office, adjacent to my computer screen and phone. This visual management was critical to our adoption as I was able to engage in many discussions with teams and individuals regarding how to breakthrough on these items. Perhaps most importantly, I started each day by looking at my Tree and Vital Few—prior to checking my 100+ e-mails and numerous voice mails. In this way, I ensured that I was serving the Vital Few first and the useful many second.

We successfully cascaded the Tree to every individual in my organization to ensure total alignment and commitment to our common goals. The one-page format was critical to the success of our cascade, particularly in the field.

Key Concepts:

1. The Success Tree is a powerful cultural tool. Mission, Vision, and Values, all best practices based on results, help shape your organization's culture. Given the importance of culture in nearly everything you do, the importance of these elements cannot be overestimated. The tree also provides an employee branch where employee satisfaction is regularly measured and improved through a closed-loop process.
2. The Success Tree favors leading indicators of employee and customer willingness to recommend over lagging financial indicators.
3. The Success Tree represents an evergreen strategic planning tool through which new data, events, and conditions can be quickly absorbed in updates (ref. evergreen tree icon).

Each key concept will be further explored and explained in the subsequent chapters on how to build your tree.

Building Your Success Tree

It is now time to get to the core of the strategy process, which I like to call "the main course," by building the top-level or "corporate" Success Tree for your organization.

1. The Tree is built on proven management theory which asserts that motivated employees lead to delighted customers and ultimately to satisfied shareholders. My mentor, Dick Palermo, often used a stool metaphor to highlight this theory.

The Stool Metaphor

A successful business or organization, when considered as a stool with three legs, would have stability or "business success" when all three legs are strong with none at the expense of another. Businesses and organizations that understand quality principles and fully adopt HPMS have clear measures and focused, closed-loop improvements for each leg of this metaphorical stool.

2. Your corporate Success Tree represents your strategy at its highest level by highlighting the "Vital Few" as compared to the "Useful Many." Back to the familiar Pareto concept, you can think of it as representative of "20% of the items that will close 80%" of your strategy gap.

3. Your Tree should be based on high quality customer, employee, and shareholder inputs, which are not translated or interpreted to more convenient options.

4. Develop your Tree with those responsible for or closest to the work rather than by a few from "on high" and, to the extent possible, it should be built on consensus as defined by "I agree to support the team's decision, even though I may not agree that the selected option is the best. I do so because my views were listened to and given fair consideration."

5. Your Tree should also be in line with the CEO and leadership team view, often via facilitation. While participative and team-based, the CEO or top leader always has the final decision.

6. Your Tree should include Values, Mission, and/or Vision— cultural and motivational best practices.

Vital Few Fundamentals

1. It's imperative that your Vital Few represent **breakthroughs** that will take your organization to new places rather than incremental improvements.

2. The Vital Few items on your Tree should receive ≅70% of your key resources.

3. Your Vital Few should be aligned to your Vision and in line with your Values and Mission.

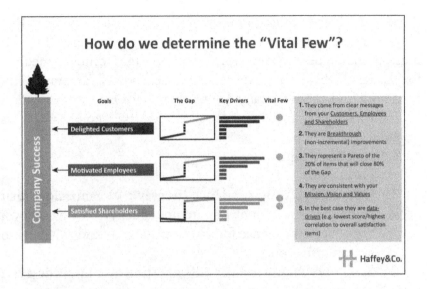

Team Stoplight Reporting

Team Stoplight Reporting is the process that connects strategy to execution, completing your closed-loop HPMS. When executed with excellence it fosters visibility, accountability and teamwork.

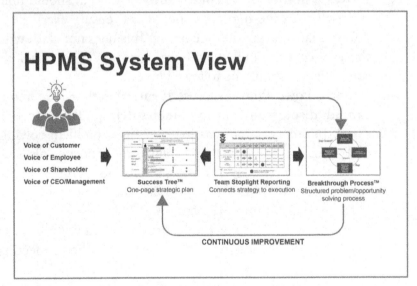

The Team Stoplight Reporting process connects all elements

A well-run Team Stoplight Reporting meeting ensures the Vital Few are getting the support and resources necessary to be successful. This meeting should be considered the most important recurring meeting for leaders, with robust discussion, decisiveness, accountability, teamwork and candor. Many of our client CEOs state that this is the only recurring meeting they attend, further emphasizing its importance.

Best practice setup:

1. **Operates at a high cadence (weekly):** Organizations that meet once a month or less are not agile. Weekly has shown to be the best cadence for assessing progress and adjusting to new information.

2. **Self-reporting:** We favor self-reporting over inspection as a concept. By having rigorous inspection, leaders will come to the meeting trying to minimize damage rather than to use the meeting to get help and alignment. Some inspection is necessary; however, teams should always side on the less-is-more approach.

3. **Drives visibility and accountability:** The team should hold themselves to the highest standard and ensure everyone is doing what they say they are doing. This does not clash with the self-reporting bullet; but once someone says they will do something, it should be followed up on.

4. **Is not a PowerPoint "success theater;" rather it is about candid discussion and problem-solving:** This meeting should be more about discussion, consensus, problem-solving, and decision-making than about aesthetically pleasing PowerPoint presentations that intend to paint a pretty picture for management, often hiding the true problems and opportunities for improvement.

5. **Is attended by 100% of the leadership team as this is the most important meeting in the company:** When a meeting is only attended by a portion, decisions cannot be made and continue to propagate the informal channels and waste associated with many existing programs. The meeting should also be inclusive, often bringing in teams working on the Vital Few for discussion.

Team Stoplight Report: Tracking the Vital Few

Ticket	Team Leader	1 Build Approach	2 Current State	3 Desired State	4 Execution Status	Intial Measure	Current Measure	Desired Measure
Rapid Adoption Process	Marry Smith	⬟				XXXXXXX	XXXXXXX	
Policies, Processes, Procedure Improvement	John Doe	➡	➡	⬇		XXXXXXX	XXXXXXX	XXXXXXX
Patient Throughput	Sam Jones	➡	➡	➡	⬟	XXXXXXX	XXXXXXX	XXXXXXX

➡ On plan / on track

⬇ Some danger of schedule, cost or quality slippage

⬟ Schedule, cost, or quality slippage imminent... leadership intervention needed

Team Stoplight Report Example

Your company's team Stoplight Report should be formatted using the same customer, employee, and financial framework as reflected in your Success Tree. Some clients elect to include their Vision and Values at the top of the weekly report to further embed these principles in your system. Many organizations include additional key performance indicators (KPIs) such as revenue, margins, cash, and backorders. All should indicate clear owners for each line item and green, yellow, or red status based on these definitions:

ICON	PROGRESS	EXPECTED ACTION
GREEN	Things are generally on track to achieve the intended targets	Continue to provide updates on progress
YELLOW	Things are off-track, but have resources in place to bring back on track	Provide visibility to the mitigation plan and updated leadership more frequently
RED	Unlikely to meet the intended targets without significant help	**Leadership intervention is needed** to support the team and bring the project back on track
◆	The initiative is complete or on-hold	No further action required

Red isn't simply a status indicator—it's a call to action! This is where leadership can and should step in to marshal resources, remove constraints, and support problem-solving.

Now that we have established the action levels needed for the project, let's discuss what should result from these discussions. If everyone just looked at a red dashboard and said, "Well, that's too bad" and went about their day, the meeting would be worthless. Here are the distinct actions recommended when something turns up yellow or red:

- Approval of a plan or resources: Leadership drives confidence in the plan or allocates needed resources. This could include "moving the goalposts" when a project is incapable of meeting the original targets.
- Intervention: Leadership could build a team to review the issue and come back with the root cause and recommendations at a specified date.
- No action: Leadership continues to let the project run and act at a later time.

As you can imagine, meetings that continuously result in "no action" are not value-added. People find meetings ineffective when there are many updates yet no approvals, support or leadership intervention. Not every meeting needs this, but practitioners should continually assess the meeting quality and adjust.

Agenda

We recommend starting with a simplified agenda and building in complexity as needed. Having no structure can lead to unproductive conversations that drive no understanding or behavior. Having too much structure leads people to focus too much on the mechanics and rush through the agenda rather than taking the time to resolve issues. Here are the topics to cover and approximate time allocation for a typical meeting:

- (10%) Hot topics: What pressing items should we cover first? These might be Vital Few items; for instance, if there was a major earthquake, get that off everyone's minds, even if it is to call a separate meeting to discuss.
- (60%) Vital Few: What items are at risk or off-track? Use most of the meeting to discuss items that need help. Teams that are green love to share their positive progress, but we must first address the areas of need.
- (15%) Vital Few needs for green items: Discuss upcoming or accomplished milestones and recognize great teamwork.
- (5%) Review last meetings action items: Maintain accountability of the team by calling out uncompleted actions and identifying next steps.
- (5%) Recap actions from the meeting: Make sure everyone is crystal clear on the next steps.
- (5%) Closing comments: Before everyone rushes out the door, give room for anyone to add final thoughts or concerns.

Driving The Culture At Team Stoplight Report Meetings

In addition to the agenda, consider grounding the conversation in your company's Values, Vision. This is the best meeting to imprint these. Consider starting the meeting with role model examples and recognition. Some groups give five minutes at the beginning of the meeting to cover this, while others allow it to flow organically. In either approach, the most important thing is to bring them up regularly (every other meeting or so). If it feels underutilized, leadership should discuss a course of action to improve.

Don't Forget The Main Point Of This Meeting: Teamwork!

Having all the processes in the world doesn't make up for people not cooperating and working together to make the business successful. Leaders should not lose sight of this. If meetings become unproductive, see who can politically maneuver their way out of things best or hide valuable information to avoid the spotlight; then consider holding a team meeting to fix that first.

Common Questions

Below is a list of common pitfalls and potential fixes:

1. What do I do if my stoplight is mostly red and yellow items? The stoplight report shows where urgency and resources are needed. If the entire stoplight report is red and yellow, the team can get overwhelmed and disengage. No one wants to go to work each day and see they are failing everywhere.
   a. Short-term fix: Help find a path toward stabilization—should we reassess our targets and move a few? Ensure that each red and yellow item has a clear path with a date to complete.
   b. Long-term fix: Consider how you got to this point to prevent it from happening again. Did you set too many goals or were they too ambitious?
2. There is a plan to get a red to a green, but it will take three months. What status should it be? The Stoplight report is intended to indicate where focus and support are needed rather than overall status. If you have a solid plan to return the project on track, consider what behavior is needed. If you need to monitor at a level of green, move it to green. Except in rare circumstances, you will want to find a path leadership can agree on and track against that to get out of red, so you can focus the energy on other escalations.
3. There is so much to discuss, how do I keep my meeting from running over each time?
   a. Assign a moderator—One person should organize the meeting and keep things on track. They must have the courage to speak up when things are off track.
   b. Take things offline—This is normal meeting etiquette, but if a topic will take more than fifteen minutes to discuss, it should have its own meeting.
   c. Get coaching for ineffective communicators—every company has meeting killers who overshare and waste time. Consider the memo approach taken by Amazon, where the presenter prepares a memo that summarizes the update and recommended action as a pre-read.

How a Team Stoplight Reporting Process

Changed the Course of Ford Motor Company

Most people see status meetings as dry, dull, low-value uses of time. In this example from Ford Motor Company, you'll see how these meetings are meant to add value and are a critical element of success.

Alan Mulally, who was CEO from 2006 to 2014, used a stoplight process called the Business Plan Review (BPR). This process was the centerpiece to the transformation, which turned Ford around in the mid-2000s and added $53 billion in shareholder value. Many of the items listed below come from the The American Icon by Bryce G. Hoffman, who shares leadership's account of Ford's incredible turnaround.

Before Mulally joined, the culture at Ford was described like this: "Meetings were political theater; side discussions (were) where the real business of the company was conducted." Leaders did not find value and focused on positioning themselves to have the least pain inflicted on them as possible.

Mulally had successfully utilized the BPR process at Boeing and knew that having a functioning governance process was critical to turning Ford around. In his BPR, which he held a 7 a.m. every Thursday, Mulally and his team would use data and facts to drive discussion and continuous improvement. He utilized the same red, yellow, green scheme highlighted in our Stoplight Reporting Process. All red items were given special attention review (SAR) in real time/same day. Through SAR, he took leadership intervention to a new level.

In the early days of rolling the BPR out at Ford, while the company was having one of the worst years in their history, Mulally found that every executive was showing green status and everything was good in their area. Mulally asked the group: "We're going to lose billions of dollars this year. Is there anything that's not going well here?" Imagine being on a sinking ship and having each department say that their group is fine!

It took the courage of Mark Fields, then head of America's, to share that one of his items was red. Despite Mark and his peer's concerns that he would be fired, Mark was recognized and supported with his red item. Weeks later, many of the leaders began to share the real status. Mulally knew the team was finally getting somewhere, and, with everything out in the open, could fix the woes affecting Ford. The leadership team became much more productive, allocated resources, and made decisions on the toughest areas affecting the company.

Mulally described his BPR as "continuous improvement of strategy and execution," perhaps the best definition of a process that regularly reviews the essential things (strategy) and how well you are performing against them (execution). The BPR gave the executive team a forum to build a culture of honesty and accountability and ensured resources were applied to the right areas of the business.

Cascading Functional, Departmental and Individual Success Trees

Now that you've completed your top-level or corporate Success Tree, it's time to further align your people, processes, and resources to your strategy through the cascade process.

The cascade process is defined as the steps taken to breakdown the company, department, and individual strategies into tangible and relevant goals for each individual. One of our experienced HPMS practitioners, John Berdahl, likens the benefits to a well-run football team where everyone knows how to play their part within a well-defined system to ensure the win.

While cascading is typically done for financial goals, we rarely see the same level of rigor taken with major company initiatives or looking to see if we are optimally utilizing our resources. All too often we see each department set their goals in a vacuum. An example tradeoff: Does the operations team need five engineers to work on a $100,000 cost savings or should the resources be used to support an earlier launch of a $100 million revenue product line? Often these conversations are not held because everyone is focused on their individual metrics rather than working with their peers to do what is best for the business.

Deming spoke frequently about the danger of optimizing individual functions at the expense of the whole.

> "Management's job is to optimize the entire system. Suboptimization is costly. It would be poor management, for example, to optimize sales, or to optimize manufacture, design of product, or of service, or incoming supplies, to the exclusion of the effect on other stages of production."
>
> —W. Edwards Deming

Many of you who've worked in traditional siloed organizations have likely suffered the effects of functional optimization over system optimization. To optimize the system, however, you first must be able to visualize it through the cascade process as well as through Stop Light Reporting.

This chapter will walk you through the basics to setting effective goals for the organization. Topics include:

1. definitions and effective goal-setting practices
2. level 1: cross-functional alignment at the senior leadership level
3. level 2: cross-functional alignment in the middle levels of the organization
4. level 3: building an individual contributor's Success Tree
5. putting the Tree to work—visual management and adjustments

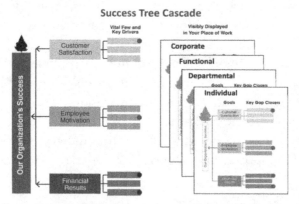

Cascade to Functional, Departmental, and Individual Levels

Definitions and effective goal-setting practices

Let's start with some definitions:

1) **Vital Few:** These are the items found on the corporate Tree. We use this term to denote the highest priority initiatives in the company. Not everyone will have goals on their Success Tree that directly impact the Vital Few.

2) **SMART Goals:** This is a widely used framework that helps improve the quality of goals. There are variations to the definition, but we use this:

   a. Specific: It should be clear what you are trying to do with little room for interpretation.

   b. Measurable: The goal should be trackable, so we know if it was successful.

   c. Achievable: It should be reasonable. It is okay to make stretch goals, but there still should be a good chance of succeeding.

   d. Relevant: The goal should clearly connect to the success of the business.

   e. Time-bound: There should be a set time for the results to occur.

3) **Vertical Alignment:** Ensuring that goals are aligned within an individual function. For example, ensuring the VP, directors, managers, and individual contributors within IT have goals that align and generally roll up together.

Benchmarking John Doerr, legenday VC and author of *Measure What Matters*

Legendary venture capitalist John Doerr, an early investor in Amazon, Google and many other successes, dedicated an entire book to the importance of a well-constructed goal setting process. See this excerpt for some further insight on this important topic:

> "By definition, objectives are significant, concrete, action oriented, and (ideally) inspirational. When properly designed and deployed, they're a vaccine against fuzzy thinking—and fuzzy execution. Effective KRs [Key Results] are specific and time-bound, aggressive yet realistic. Most of all, they are measurable and verifiable.
>
> John Doer, Chairman at Kleiner Perkins

More on Goals

While SMART format is a very intuitive concept, it is rarely utilized properly in most companies. Why? Because the act of goal-setting is both an attempt to predict the future *and* create structure where previously none existed. There often is no black and white, but many shades of gray, making goal-setting just as much of an art as a science. For that reason, the SMART format is not a hard and fast rule, as early on, the team may not yet know their Desired State yet. In other cases, there are no existing measures to assess performance, and creating the measure may be more trouble than the benefit.

This can also be a key to empowering teams to set the desired performance levels. W. Edwards Deming believed you should avoid telling the teams the answer, allowing the data and their imagination to guide this. While a great practice, we have found that for some projects this can lead to unnecessary swirl, where the senior leaders are already clear on where they want to go and leave the team trying to read their minds.

The Myth of "We Have to Do Everything!"

We often have employees who scoff at the idea of putting only three to five goals on their Tree. They argue that they have fifty things to do, and if even one isn't accomplished, there will be significant issues. An immediate counterargument is that you would never put a goal of showing up to work or reading e-mail, right? There are always tasks that are implied as part of just doing your job. If we wrote out everything we did and tracked it, the system would not be effective. Instead, we focus on a few goals that are the largest drivers of our company's success.

Another way to think about it is that there is often a spectrum of results to deliver. In school, we could complete an assignment, but receive anywhere from an A to an F. A C grade was considered passing. Using this concept in business, our top three to five projects are the ones we need an A or A+ on, while the other projects can get by with a C grade. It is usually impossible in a world of finite resources to get an A+ on every task.

One last view—if we continue to say everything is important, nothing is important. We *must* prioritize because focusing on everything will likely lead to failure.

Laura Vanderkam, an author and speaker, gives a great example of how this concept is put into practice. She explains how everyone is very busy, but if your water heater failed at your home and you needed to find seven hours in your week to get it fixed, you would. Time is fluid and we will always make time for our top priorities even if it comes at the expense of other items. Treat your top goals like that broken water heater.

The Myth of the Annual Goal-Setting Process

A funny thing happens when we present this concept to a conservative company, telling them that Trees can be updated regularly as conditions change. Many are adamant that you set goals at the beginning of the year and rank performance against them. They believe if you allow people to adjust during the year, they will all try to get out of their commitments and set easier goals.

There is a disastrous element to this in most companies that cannot predict the future one year from now, let alone three to six months from now. While setting goals for a year is comforting, it is based on the illusion of control. Things can change so rapidly that leaving goals alone all year, or even six months, is far too long and will lead people to work on the wrong things. In many leading tech companies, such as Google, goals are set in three-month waves and accelerated the annual review to four times per year.

To the concern about people getting out of their goals, there is a reason companies pay a lot of money to have middle level management. These individuals are often responsible for the original annual goals, so you should trust their judgement when making mid-year course-corrections. No amount of (fake) control will make up for poor managers. Focus on having the right people rather than bureaucratic controls.

I bring this concept up because people should know their Tree is living and evergreen, as such new events, information, and accomplishments are quickly absorbed in updates. If unattended, it quickly becomes outdated and loses its many benefits. Goals can and will change when new data is available or the situation or environment changes.

Cross-Functional Horizontal Alignment

For most organizations, the first step in the cascade process is to ensure horizontal alignment at the functional level. This is generally accomplished through these steps:

1. Each functional leader constructs a draft copy of their Tree for presentation.
2. The leaders get together to review each function of the Tree and discuss where partnership is needed and direct resources to bottlenecks. Trees are then finalized and sent through their individual functions (see next section).

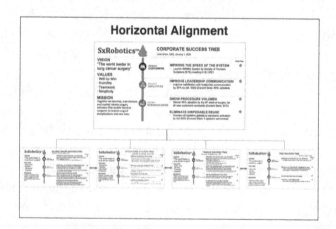

Horizontal Alignment of Sales, Operations, Finance, and R&D
(note: SxRobotics is a fictitious company)

Powerful discussions and negotiations often come at this step. For example, sales may have built their plan on having a new product at a certain time, but unless that new product is reflected in their R&D and operations colleagues' Trees, the program could be at risk. The overall objective is to develop and agree on unified team goals to ensure alignment and high performance. Too often, we see organizations that don't incorporate a process like this resulting in disparate goals, poor alignment, and poor execution. The bottom line: Take the time to do this step. Your employees will appreciate it, and your customers and shareholders will benefit from it.

Vertical Alignment

In larger organizations, vertical alignment to the department or individual level constitutes the majority of the effort behind your cascade process. This generally starts by linking functional, department, and individual goals to your Vital Few.

One refrain we often hear goes like this: "I don't have anything to do with the Vital Few therefore, this system is not for me." This is a form of change resistance and must be addressed early and often in your HPMS journey. It's best for individuals with no direct link to the Vital Few to start with their activities and work up, i.e., "strategy down, activity up" and make the broader connections to Customer Satisfaction, Employee Motivation and Financial Success.

Individual Goals

While we covered how a function would align within itself, we all know that each role has its unique relationships. A few important notes about individual contributor Trees:

1. Many individual contributors will likely have no link to the Vital Few, and that's okay. The most important part for individual Trees is not how they link to the Vital Few but rather how their work connects to the organization's key stakeholders. If an organization focuses too much at this

level on linkage to the Vital Few, individuals will feel like their work isn't important, which is far from the truth!

2. Initiatives are difficult to place on a given branch of the Tree. Individuals should focus more on their three to five top goals rather than worry about filling up each branch. Goals can be placed on the branch they best fit.

3. Many individuals' goals are not based on initiatives, but the continued performance of their duties, which may be highly variable based on business needs. SMART goals may become difficult at this level, though still possible.

As you can see at this level, setting goals at the individual contributor level takes a different approach. Ensure the priorities are clear and linked to the greater company's success. Note that all Trees in your cascade should reflect the organization's Vital Few regardless of whether the individual's goals line up directly. This ensures that everyone knows the company's strategy and can support it.

Visual Management and "Working" Trees

As mentioned previously, it's critical that your Tree be visible in your area of work and serve as a touchstone before you begin your day's activities. Query if your activities line up with the Vital Few and are in line with your Vision, Mission, and Values on a daily basis. While awkward at first, you can develop this into a powerful habit: Vital Few first, emails and phone calls second!

We already use visual management in several areas of our lives to manage our behavior, such as placing a Post-it note with a reminder of an important task on our desk. Visual management has also been utilized significantly in manufacturing plants for decades.

Strong visual management also ensures continuous improvement of alignment throughout the organization as disconnects are visible and can be addressed. This is such an important aspect for some leaders that they insist on it and hold their organizations accountable to this practice.

Cascaded Success Trees are not marketing materials and do not need to be perfectly formatted. Content is far more important than appearance. It's more important to simply use your Tree in discussions and meetings. When practiced in this way, you have a "working Tree" that you may carry with you in the factory and the field. You may even mark it up to cross off items you have executed or add or modify existing Key Drivers.

Visible Working Success Tree example

I strongly encourage you to think about how you can provide all new employees with a Tree on their first day of work. This could be broken down as a thirty-day Tree reflecting the key activities you'd like the new employee to focus on during their onboarding, in your own handwriting. For example:

Customer Branch	Visit two key customers
Employee Branch	Complete all training and onboarding coursework
Financial Branch	Understand the company's financial statements, shareholder expectations, and profit drivers

Once that's complete, you can take their Tree up to the next level. The key here is that you are showing its importance and utility from day one.

FAQs

How often should you update your Tree?
The simplest answer is that Trees should be updated when they are
no longer relevant. For some individuals, adjusting trees monthly is
normal, while another individual may have the same goals all year. It
depends on the nature of your work and the rate of change. As with
the recent COVID-19 disease, everyone's goals were upended when
quarantines occurred. The existing Trees were no longer relevant
and updated with several of our clients. This is an extreme case, but
individuals may experience significant events that require adjustments.

How do you recommend updating your Tree? (e.g., manager
approval, functions, when a goal changes).
For individuals, we recommend manager approval. A one-on-one
discussion should cover the original target, what changed, and what
the recommendation is now.

If I don't have an item linked to the Vital Few, am I not important?
I had to mention this again since it comes up so often! Every
employee has a part to play in an organization. The Vital Few drive
the top priorities for the success of the future business. Most individuals work on tasks that keep the business functioning today, which
without them, there would be no future business. The Tree is about
more than the Vital Few. It's as much about your Mission, Vision,
and Values as well as the framework provided by the branches
themselves. I can't imagine an employee that can't be connected to
the customer, their teammates, or organization's financial health.

CHAPTER 8

PRINCIPLE 6: FLEXING YOUR PROBLEM-SOLVING MUSCLES

In 1854 in Westminster, England, there were waves of sickly individuals flooding the infirmaries. No one could explain this sudden surge as the death toll mounted. Scientists and physicians argued over potential sources. Was it spread in the air, food, or by other means? A few months later, after hundreds died, the cases stopped after a water pump handle was removed. This wasn't just a hunch, good luck, or a political decision but based on empirical evidence and scientific thinking. John Snow, a surgeon, brought the cause to light—he mapped where each case originated and found something startling. The cases were all grouped around one intersection in the city, which coincided with the location of a community water pump. Thousands of lives were saved, and this case became famous for the power of empirical evidence and data analysis. It also significantly influenced public health and sanitation projects in the early 1900s.

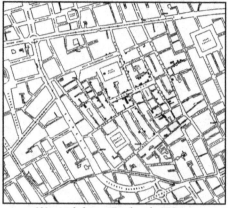

Westminister, England, 1824

A map of the 1854 Broad Street outbreak. The dark bars indicate where most cases were found. As you can see, the cases were grouped around one neighborhood, which resulted from a contaminated water source at the center.

The Scientific Method

The scientific method can be credited for the vast majority of the technologies we use today and is also the ancestor of virtually all problem-solving methodologies today. It is why there are planes in the sky, why we are living longer than ever due to modern medicine, and why many businesses flourish.

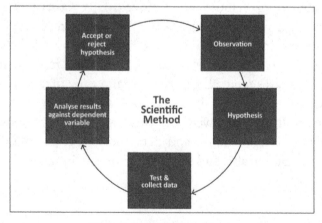

The Scientific Method

How does this apply to your business? While you may not be dealing with disease outbreaks or planning a mission to Mars, using structured methodologies to understand a problem and devise a solution can be equally powerful in focusing your finite resources to accomplish great things more effectively and efficiently than through opinion and experience alone. Your business has hundreds, if not thousands, of opportunities and problems waiting to be solved.

Imagine if you competed against a company with an identical workforce selling an identical product. The only difference is that your business is full of talented people exceptional at problem-solving and execution. You can imagine how over a few months or years you would be poised to outmaneuver and grow beyond your competitor.

The auto industry has examples of this, where over a few decades, Toyota rose to prominence and created a lower cost, higher quality automobile than the US manufacturer. This didn't happen magically, nor did Japan have more resources than the US (in fact, they had fewer). Toyota's success was attributed to the application of quality principles and the use of Deming's PDCA problem-solving methodology.

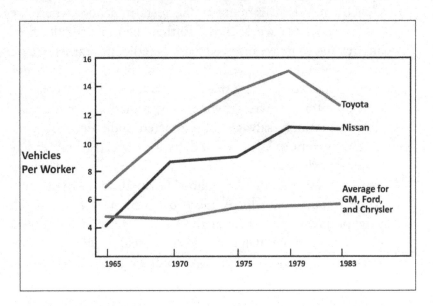

Efficiency of Toyota and Nissan Plants: this trend shows vehicles per worker and illustrates why they are able to provide lower-cost vehicles to the consumer.[5]

Which Methodology to Use

Before we get into what we recommend, it's important to know that there are several methods available, each with unique advantages and disadvantages. Most individuals in manufacturing are familiar with PDCA, DMAIC, and a host of other tools. Rather than debate which one is the best, let's start with the benefits associated with having *any* common process:

1. Identify what to focus on first: All organizations have a limited capacity to do breakthrough work and should stage areas of focus over time. Rather than try to do everything and fail, the goal is to "eat the elephant one bite at a time." This applies to HPMS as a whole, but specifically for the Breakthrough Process—we need to break down an opportunity into pieces.

2. Coaching: We all remember the tests in school where we had to show our work, right? Rather than just see the final answer and score we received partial credit and learned where we went wrong when we had to explain our thought process. This applies to business projects too; teams can be coached on where they go wrong when using a methodology. Often, the project can be salvaged or redirected, and everyone grows.

3. Communication: With a standard language, it is immensely easier for everyone to share progress, ask for input, and receive approval. It is similar to following an instruction manual when building an IKEA piece of furniture—you can tell your progress by looking at the page number. If there were no instruction manual, it would be difficult to communicate how far along and what you are doing next.

---

5 (Source: https://sloanreview.mit.edu/article/manufacturing-innovation-lessons-from-the-japanese-auto-industry/)

4. Proven track record: The modern methodologies used and recommended here have been utilized for decades and have generated significant results.
5. Speed: When organizations utilize a common problem-solving process, language, and tools, they can execute more rapidly and with more confidence than organizations that use a variety of these items.

The Breakthrough Process™ and Job Tickets

Now that it should be clear why a process can be helpful, let's discuss the benefits of the Breakthrough Process. The most important advantage of our process is that it is far more intuitive and has a lower barrier of entry to implement in organizations. Lean and Six Sigma are fantastic, but they are packed with statistical concepts and often complicate things (e.g. the proficiency system developed with yellow, green, and black belts. As a leading Lean practitioner and Wiremold Company CEO, Art Byrne put it:

> "I am running a business, not a karate class."
>
> —Art Byrne, former President and CEO of Wiremold

Additionally, there are complicated mechanisms to certify a business, and before you know it, the business is improving at Lean for the sake of improving at Lean, rather than giving the organization flexibility to focus on the business needs.

With this in mind, the likelihood that a sales or service representative in the field using it is next to zero. Again, we believe that Lean and Six Sigma tools have their place and are highly beneficial, but most organizations will benefit more from a system that can be adopted by everyone rather than the system with the most tools and features.

We have found that the most experienced practitioners of other systems quickly adopt the Breakthrough Process once they understand that it utilizes the same powerful "DNA", though packaged and communicated in a simpler form.

There are four steps to the Breakthrough Process, which we will cover in detail:

1) Build the approach: lay the foundation for the team by outlining the opportunity.
2) Define the Current State: baseline the way things are and assess the levers available for improvement.
3) Define the Desired State: build an aspirational target and plan to achieve the target.
4) Execute, iterate, and monitor: turn the plan into action, adjust as necessary, and track progress.

Breakthrough Process™

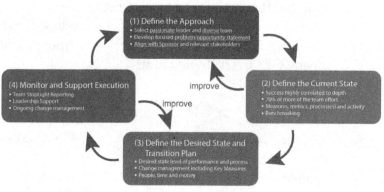

"The major problem we face is not any particular problem. It is the process we use to solve problems." - Steven Covey

The Breakthrough Process

Step 1: Build the approach

Imagine you were commissioned to build an elevator in your building. Imagine how successful you would be if:

1) You didn't clearly understand what you were building the elevator for, whether for freight or a few people.
2) The project manager had a separate, full-time job and wasn't too interested in completing this project.
3) You had no electricians on the team to wire it.

4) You didn't have a schedule for when you work and how you would accomplish the build.

While this example seems absurd (of course, this project would fail!), I have observed myriad business projects start without taking the time to build their approach.

The first step in the 4-step process requires teams to define the work before they set off to solve the problem to save time and energy.

Here are the primary requirements to complete this step:

1. Define the problem or opportunity clearly and concisely. It is amazing how many projects underestimate this step. Often, we find wildly different interpretations of what the team should accomplish. Sometimes the project is canceled after realizing we don't even know why or what we are solving.

2. Select a passionate team leader. We like to say there are three requirements for the team leader: 1) passion for the problem or opportunity, 2) passion for the problem or opportunity, and 3) passion for the problem or opportunity. Then look for the right skills on the team. The leader should be able to dedicate up to 100% of their effort to the project. If nothing else, the leader's job is to drive energy into this project and mobilize the team.

3. Gather the right team members. Teams will not succeed without having the right skill sets available to the team. Experience is a good starting point but not the only thing to look for. Sometimes it can be detrimental to the project as some are convinced that they've tried everything already. Strive for a diverse, cross-functional, and cross-layer team populated by people willing to look at the problem or opportunity differently than in the past. Team members should be able to dedicate up to 50% of their effort to the project.

4. Select an executive sponsor. Your team should consist of a sponsor who can help guide the team, assist with resources, and remove constraints. Ideally, the sponsor can gain approval for the team's plan. An active sponsor should be able to dedicate up to 10% of their effort to the project.

5. Develop a team process. You will want to lay out the project approach and how often you will meet. Many times, projects are accomplished in one day, one week or one month sprints to develop a proposal. You don't need to make it overly complicated but plan upfront and leave more time than necessary. It's always easy to cut back time but adding more on top of busy people's schedules is tough. If you do this right, you will see constraints pop up early—the star team member may be unavailable for half the project, requiring you to adjust. Do this now rather than mid-project.

6. Define the approach. Through experience, we have found that projects fall into these three categories.

   a. **Root cause analysis:** A project that will require significant problem-solving. Start here if you have a limited understanding of what you want to solve. The 1854 Broad Street outbreak is a good example of this, as are manufacturing problems.

   b. **Process overhaul/creation:** This is a project where you know that the existing process is insufficient, and building a new process is the single greatest aspect of the future state. Sales processes are great examples of this, where we know that alignment of best practices and consistency will drive the most significant improvement.

   c. **Just do it:** Some projects have predefined endpoints, and the purpose of the project team is to figure out how it will be accomplished. Typically, this involves a Current State understanding of the available levers. An example is shown below, where a client had to turn their EBITDA from -\$10 million/month to breakeven.

Stating where the project lands can align the stakeholders and team on the best approach. For instance, if we are "Just do it," we can't expect the teams to dwell on why we are where we are as much as understanding and weighing the opportunities. If we are doing a process overhaul, we know that a major part of the Current State needs to include process mapping and benchmarking. The project type can change as you gain information, but it helps to plan this early in the project.

We recommend that this information, along with the expected approach in steps two to four, be written out on a one-page Job Ticket. This document should be continually reviewed and updated as the project progresses and should represent the "one source of truth" for where the project is along the journey.

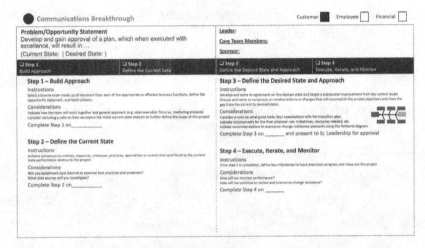

Job Ticket example

This document writes out the planned approach in one page. It is not meant to be inclusive of everything, and it will likely change over time. In addition to a clear problem/opportunity statement for the team, here are two recommendations to include in this charter:

1. **Forecasted dates for completing each step of the Breakthrough Process:** Some teams have been uneasy about including dates since they are worried they may change. The purpose of dates is to at least track against the latest thinking, i.e., is the project progressing slower or faster than originally expected? Most important is having a defined step three date and booking time on senior leaders' calendars to review. This makes the project more real to the team and sets an urgency.

2. **Considerations for each step:** Using the Pareto principle concept, what are the few items the team should consider

in the approach of each step? This not only stretches the thinking of the team, but it also gives stakeholders a view into the approach and allows for constructive feedback. An example for step two could be a note on the top two or three most important data sources the team will look at; in step three, what are expectations that must be considered?

This document can be adjusted as the project progresses but should always be considered the "one source of truth" for the latest high-level approach the team is taking.

A Bit More On The Team Process

We have all been on ineffective teams. Here are some best practices to consider:

Shorter, more frequent meetings are more effective. We always have found that the most productive team time is right before or right after the team meeting. It's human behavior to ignore things that aren't pressing and to procrastinate. Use that to your advantage by meeting more frequently. Consider starting with meeting daily or three times a week and dialing back from there. It's okay to have meetings that are fifteen minutes long sometimes; just cut it short and move on with your day.

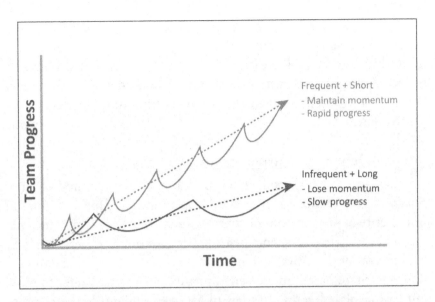

Face to face day-long intensives are great for heavy lifting. In Lean, the term is Kaizen, where the group gets together for a day or multiple days to focus on a project. Most teams find these face-to-face sprints the most productive of the whole project.

Define roles and rules upfront. Consider selecting a notetaker, timekeeper, and clarify the use of phones and laptops in working meetings. Don't go overboard. I saw one group give everyone a role, and the team spent more time focused on their role than on the project!

Leave your functional hat behind. And be prepared to do some real work as a team. While you may come from finance, your role on the Job Ticket team is likely to expand beyond that and all should be willing to get their hands dirty - especially in the Current State.

Bottom line: There is a lot that can go into planning a project. The purpose is not to burden the team but accelerate them. Rather than throw every tool at the project, identify a few that will make it more successful than past projects. Being the leader of a project is all about driving energy and creating an environment to do the work, so it isn't unusual for one to spend a lot of time thinking about step one.

Step 2: Define the Current State

In this step, you will collect the building blocks required to draw insights and identify future state opportunities. This is often the most critical step in the journey; as such, you should go "insanely deep", be prepared to spend 70% to 80% of your effort here. This step can be counterintuitive to some as they believe they understand the Current State based on convenient assumptions and prefer to move on to the plan. Teams that fail to go deep enough here are prone to failure and disappointment. John Snow couldn't have solved the cholera outbreak if he did not know why it was caused. This can be found in business processes too; without understanding why things work, we cannot improve.

> "Every system is perfectly designed to get the result that it does." "You don't know what you don't know."
>
> —W. Edwards Deming

W. Edwards Deming's quotes above are a great argument for the Current State; whatever we are doing now is leading to the results we are getting today. If we don't understand what we are doing and what is influencing the system, it is nearly impossible to improve and predict future performance.

Another important factor in the Current State is the need to be candid about current performance and not take things personally. Dick Palermo would emphasize the need for candor in this step with this statement:

> "If the Current State is ugly, let it be ugly."
>
> Dick Palermo

If an organization sugarcoats the Current State, they will not see the gap correctly and therefore be unable to solve it. In some cases, we amplify the Current State gap and concerns because that is the only way things will be addressed.

Here Are The Primary Requirements For This Step:

1. Articulate the Current State: This could be done through process maps or root cause analysis, and it is where you simplify the main drivers of the current performance level. The current performance should be defined by measures and metrics where possible.

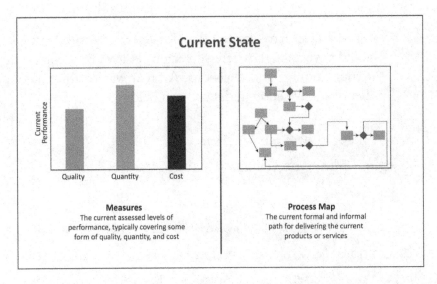

2. Benchmark: Often, we can derive understanding of things by looking at others who have gone before us. This could be an internal benchmark of someone who performs significantly better than we do, or it could be an external benchmark of a company considered best in class. In either case, it is important to start with a "best" result and the context of that result, not just something that looks shiny.

"Benchmarking should always start with a result."

—Bernie Haffey

3. Identify improvement opportunities: These are the building blocks for step three where you will lay out the levers that can adjust performance in the future. Typically, you will use data or consensus to Pareto the top opportunities. Consider each opportunity as a lever for impacting performance—some levers will be large and some will be small. In addition to the size of the levers, the ability to pull the lever will be different for each. This step identifies the levers that are the longest and easiest to pull or the best mix of both.

You will never have enough data for a perfect answer, but you should have enough where you can be at least 80% confident in your findings and decisions. A great way to think about when you have enough data shown below.

Don't wait for all the information

(Excerpt from The Amazon Management System by R. Charan, 2019)

"In war, when timing is even more critical, former U.S. Secretary of State and retired four-star general Colin Powell advocated a 40-70 rule: if you have less than 40% of the information, you shouldn't make a decision. But if you wait until you have more than 70% of the information, you have waited too long. Once the information is in the 40-70 range, go with your gut.

In business, Bezos used a 70-90 rule instead. He stated that "Most decisions should probably be made with somewhere around 70% of the information you wish you had. If you wait for 90%, in most cases, you're probably being slow. Plus, either way, you need to be good at quickly recognizing and correcting bad decisions. If you're good at course-correcting, being wrong may be less costly than you think, whereas being slow is going to be expensive for sure."

Bottom line: By the end of this step, the most important part is gaining consensus of the empowered, cross-functional team. It won't be perfect, but if you do it right, you will be better equipped to make a decision than if you skipped it.

Step 3: Define the Desired State

Now that you have assessed why things are the way they are and collected the relevant levers, you get to do the fun part of dreaming up an exciting future state and setting milestones to get there. If we are building an elevator, this would mean we have collected the measurements, performance requirements, and potential systems to install and need to decide what we will install, the cost of the full project, and the timeline to implement. In some cases, the Desired State is dictated for the team—usually by the CEO and executive team.

Here are the primary requirements for this step:

1. Defined endpoint: We must have a measurable and time-defined target. The clearer, the better. Sometimes teams miss this step, start doing tasks, and realize they are rudderless and far away from the originally intended target. Don't do this. Typically, this endpoint is a stretch or aspirational goal. This goal should be explored creatively but grounded by the knowledge gained in step two.

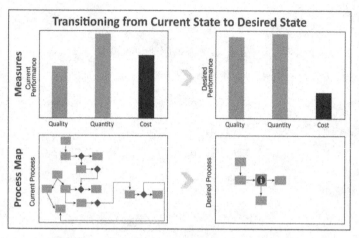

Desired State Process, Technology, and Performance

2. Clear milestones and resource needs: While we wouldn't expect a full project plan defined for each work day, we would expect high-level milestones that demonstrate progress to the endpoint. Typically, the first 30, 60, and 90 days are well-defined, and overall costs and personnel needs are roughly defined. As the project progresses, you will run into surprises and need to adjust. That is why it is vital to not over define the plan but give some slack to adjust to. Most importantly, we have found that having dedicated resources to execute the project, who can adjust course when needed and keep executive sponsors in the loop, are far more critical than having a "perfect" plan.

3. Change management: If your project requires people to change (internal or external), you should be thoughtful about the challenges ahead. None of us change our behaviors without a fight, so we can't just communicate the change and expect it to be successful. In step four, we will use change management continuously until the project is successfully completed. See chapter 8 for a detailed description of our recommended change management fishbone diagram tool.

Pilots

We routinely deal with teams balancing the art of doing too much or too little. Telling a company to invest millions of dollars because a team spent thirty days analyzing it is scary for the teams who think that their management won't be sold, so they sometimes settle on the free option that is too conservative and won't generate any results.

A happy medium is to go with the more aggressive model, but pilot it in a focused trial. In this case, a $10 million dollar investment may only be a $500,000 investment in the next three months, which will allow the kinks to get worked out and prove or disprove the concept.

The design of this pilot should have a clear date and defined result that would be indicative of future investment. When in doubt, work with your sponsor and stakeholders to dial in the right level of investment for the project.

Bottom line: Gain consensus on a clear endpoint and waypoints to get there. This step is typically completed with approval through a stakeholder review. If you keep your stakeholders in the loop along the way, this step is usually a formality or just a matter of timing the resource needs. If you don't keep the right people in the loop, this step can become a surprise slap in the face, requiring weeks of rework.

Step 4: Execute, Iterate and Monitor

Now that the project resources are secured, the project work commences. Going back to the earlier elevator analogy, imagine we just received approval from the building owner and can get to work. For anyone that has ever done a home renovation or watched one on HGTV, you know this is only the beginning of the project and that new information will present itself, requiring you to make tradeoffs on the path forward. Will you find a structural beam behind the wall you want to knock down? It makes for good TV and for the project leader, many stressful situations.

Here are the primary requirements in this step:

1. Tracking and achievement of milestones: The team leader needs to continue to show progress on the intended plan. In unhealthy cultures, leaders will try to stay out of view and chug away, even if the project is headed for disaster and hope people will stop paying attention. In a mature HPMS company, the project leaders are emboldened to share progress, be candid when things are missed, and ask for help.

2. Monitoring and measuring progress: Not to be confused with milestones shown above, at some point, we need to transition from activity-oriented progress to business results. The project likely set out to make a measurable impact with customers, employees, or shareholders—we should drive accountability and be candid when things aren't working out as intended. We also should communicate and recognize when things are going well. The leader should have a clear date for when the project can officially close. The work may continue indefinitely, but the sprint to implement should be finite.

3. Iteration: Teams need to stay adaptable and be ready to call it when presented with new information. In some projects, things change dramatically after a few months, and assumptions need to be revisited. The sooner a team can identify that point and adjust, the less damage it will cause and create more upside opportunity. Additionally, change management barriers will begin to show up as you implement, so the team must continually adjust the approach to facilitate changing behaviors.

Bottom Line: This step requires discipline, courage to speak the truth and ask for help, and candor for indicating when the project isn't going as planned. Through strong communication, monitoring, and iteration, teams will find their way through the project. Finally, the company should recognize the hard work and what was learned, even if the results aren't there.

Wrap up of the Breakthrough Process

As you can see, there is a lot to think about when becoming involved in a project. By following the steps above, a team maximizes their odds of driving a successful outcome. By taking the project in steps, you can effectively break the problem and build it back up again without overwhelming the team. We often get a stressed newly chosen project leader who, after taking them through the first few items, sees that these projects are manageable when following this process. After completing hundreds of these we have found that, while each project is different, they all can benefit from the structure provided.

Practical application

So now that you understand the process and have seen a few examples, where to begin?

- Crawl, walk, then run. Apart from utilizing the Vital Few, try moving rapidly in a few areas. Even though a baseball swing is intuitive, you want to take a few swings at practice before going big. Do a one-hour job ticket, a one-day, and onward.
- Manage the quality of the process. Don't let it become a flavor of the month; ensure results are achieved. Be selective on what goes through the process and ensure they have a great experience and generate results before training everyone.
- Manage the timing. Parkinson's law states, "Work expands so as to fill the time available for its completion." If you say that the project is thirty days, people will take thirty days. Rather, for items that need little prework or data analysis, challenge the team to finish steps one through three in a week. In some cases, you may only need to do a one-hour project.
- Not everything has to use the Breakthrough Process. Some projects lend themselves to other processes, such as product development, which follow set steps already defined. In other cases, the solution may be obvious where we'd call it a "Just do it."

We will wrap up this chapter with a few examples that will help show the power of the application.

**Leveraging structured problem-solving
to drive market adoption**

INTRALASE®

Ron Kurtz, MD, was a second-year resident at the University of Michigan's Kellogg Eye Center in 1992 when a graduate student from Gérard Mourou's Center for Ultrafast Optical Science presented with retinal damage from a laboratory femtosecond ($\cong$10- to 15-second pulse) laser. This unfortunate encounter led to a research collaboration between Kurtz and Mourou's lab in the area of laser-tissue interactions.

While at a conference in 1994, Ron met Tibor Juhasz, PhD, Chief Scientist at San Diego start-up Intelligent Surgical Lasers (ISL). Tibor and his team were investigating picosecond ($\cong$10- to 12-second pulse) laser technology and had successfully developed a delivery system for the cornea. This encounter, which I liken to the vintage eighties Reese's commercial where the guy with a chocolate bar bumps into the gal with peanut butter, resulted in an intense collaboration at Michigan.

With seed capital and guidance from Tom Porter at EDF Ventures, Kurtz and Juhasz negotiated patent licenses and spun out from the University as IntraLase Corp. in 1997.

While myriad applications existed for the technology, the company chose to focus on creating "flaps" (a horizontal dissection of the cornea), the first step in the LASIK procedure, with more precision and safety than the current oscillating metal blade.

A year later, they moved the company to Irvine, CA, the epicenter of ophthalmic innovation. With the move, the company attracted world-class management in Randy Alexander, Eric Weinberg, and Shelly Thunen, along with top-tier ophthalmic tech venture investors Bill Link, PhD, and Gil Kliman, MD. Together they launched the world's first commercially available femtosecond laser in 2001—a true breakthrough.

In 2003, the board hired Bob Palmisano, a seasoned public company CEO, to help the company achieve the next levels of performance. Bob had previously been CEO of Summit Technology, Inc., a company that benefited greatly from HPMS, so naturally, he brought this process and a few of his senior executives with him. I was fortunate to have been one; another was Charline Gauthier, OD, PhD.

Like many novel technologies, the company faced significant market adoption challenges, the first of which was economics. We were replacing a $40,000 console with a $475,000 laser, and a $25 blade with a $150 per-eye consumable, thereby increasing a surgeon's cost per case by more than ten times. Regardless of this premium, sales got off to a good with $18 million in revenue in 2002. Sales slowed in 2003, below investor expectations; in addition, and more concerning from a financial perspective, customers were not fully converting their LASIK volumes to the new technology.

In our first HPMS offsite strategy session together in 2003, we identified "Procedure Adoption" as the number one for our shareholders. Hence it became one of our Vital Few. Given the high priority and complex nature of the problem, we further agreed to leverage the Breakthrough Process.

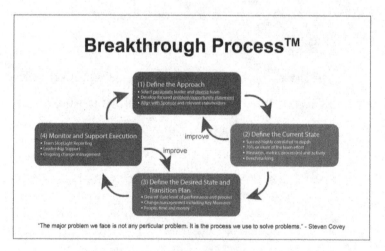

Breakthrough Process™

(1) Define the Approach
- Select passionate leader and diverse team
- Develop focused problem/opportunity statement
- Align with Sponsor and relevant stakeholders

(2) Define the Current State
- Success highly correlated to depth
- 70% or more of the team effort
- Measures, metrics, process(es) and activity
- Benchmarking

(3) Define the Desired State and Transition Plan
- Desired state level of performance and process
- Change management including Key Measures
- People, time and money

(4) Monitor and Support Execution
- Team StopLight Reporting
- Leadership Support
- Ongoing change management

improve

"The major problem we face is not any particular problem. It is the process we use to solve problems." - Steven Covey

4-Step Breakthrough Process

Define the Approach

Having defined the problem, our next step was to form and activate a diverse team that was passionate about the problem/opportunity. We selected teammates from each commercial function (sales, marketing, clinical applications, field service engineering, operations, finance, and IT) and various levels within the organization. We further agreed on a disciplined meeting process that would allow us to complete the project in thirty days.

Current State Analysis

As the team dug into the Current State, we first looked at our existing customer adoption rates. We learned that a third of our customers were high adopters (greater than 90% of flaps), another third were low adopters (less than 10% of flaps), and the remaining third were somewhere in between. We then looked at the activities associated with new customers and agreed we were operating at a Process Level of 1 based on this scale:

Process Maturity Levels

Level 0	No process or metric activity
Level 1	Limited process or metrics; some success achieved through management of results.
Level 2	Some process activity; potentially related processes managed as discrete activities with discrete metrics; limited or anecdotal process improvement cycles.
Level 3	Structured review of processes for effectivity; evidence of improved results through process improvement; some benchmarks used in development of processes and metrics.

Level 4	Strong evidence of improved results through connected processes; benchmarks routinely used in development of processes and metrics and periodic effectivity reviews.
Level 5	Processes, metrics, and results are identified as best in class against top-performing benchmarks; ties between process effectivity and business success are clear and understood by all; metrics are routinely used to refine and improve processes.

From there, we went insanely deep, interviewing and surveying all customers as well as the field personnel that touched them through the customer experience to identify what leads to successful or unsuccessful adoption. From the collected data and comments, we derived a few critical truths, root causes, and best internal practices.

In addition to stratified adoption levels and a low process maturity level, we learned that:

1. Physicians with a "blade on the shelf" presale expectation became high adopters. They possessed a "blade-free" vision for their practice and were willing to endure ease-of-use, speed, and reliability challenges to achieve their higher goal.

2. There was a high correlation between initial laser reliability and adoption, and the surgeon's inclination to adopt was formed in the first four surgical weeks.

3. We discovered that clinical trainers who demanded the full surgery schedule for training were much more likely to generate high adopters than those that allowed surgeons to go slowly.

The team then moved to benchmarking, specifically to the Ritz-Carlton customer-facing process, which provided a world-class framework for our Desired State.

Collaborative customer-facing process including clear escalation step...

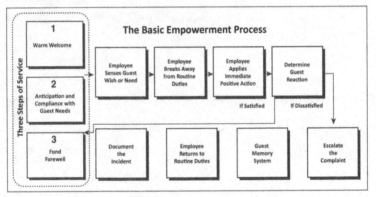

Desired State Process, Plan, and Measurement

Leveraging what we learned in Current State and benchmarking, we then mapped out a Desired State Rapid AdoptionProcess and agreed on 85% procedure adoption in thirty days as our key success measure.

We put this new process in place thirty days from the team's first meeting and, while not perfect, it was immediately effective—taking our average adoption rate from 50% to 95%—a level that was maintained globally for several years afterward.

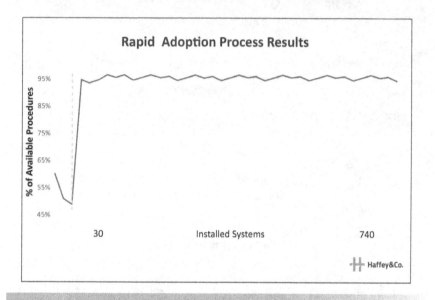

Besides solving a critical financial problem, the new team process delighted customers, with some saying they "felt like they were being served in a fine restaurant." It also improved employee satisfaction, particularly with our field service engineers, who were now part of the process.

Remarkably, this breakthrough in adoption was achieved with a process change supported by effective change management; it did not require any organizational or structural changes. This process and its results proved critical to reaching revenues of $132 million and operating profitability in 2006.

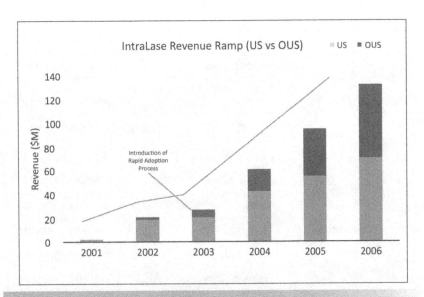

This is a powerful example of how structured problem-solving can be leveraged to improve critical processes and commercial results.

Footnote on Process Level

The Rapid Adoption process and results are considered "best-in-class" and have been used as a benchmark for numerous other companies facing market adoption challenges.

Process Maturity Levels

Level 0   No process or metric activity

Level 1   Limited process or metrics; some success achieved through management of results

Level 2   Some process activity; potentially related processes managed as discrete activities with discrete metrics; limited or anecdotal process improvement cycles

Level 3   Structured review of processes for effectivity; evidence of improved results through process improvement; some benchmarks used in development of processes and metrics

Level 4   Strong evidence of improved results through connected processes; benchmarks routinely used in development of processes and metrics and in routine effectivity reviews

Level 5   Processes, metrics, and results are identified as best in class against top-performing benchmarks; ties between process effectivity and business success are clear and understood by all; metrics are routinely used to refine and improve processes

Day-to-Day Use of a Common Problem-Solving Process and Language

I've written about the power of the Breakthrough Process applied to your organization's largest opportunities or Vital Few. If application of structured problem-solving stops there, however, you haven't done enough to establish the quality-based culture and understanding necessary for HPMS and your organization to succeed. From experience, I recommend that all problems and opportunities in the enterprise be approached with this common problem-solving process and these simple terms:

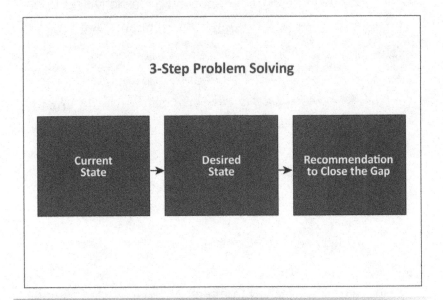

When driven down into your organization, this will allow HPMS principles to touch all employees. More importantly, it will improve the quality and speed of decisions from the boardroom to the reception desk. In many cases it can be executed verbally – also known as a "Verbal Job Ticket".

Let's consider an example of how we applied this simple, verbal (no PowerPoint!) process at Summit Technology, Inc. When I started in 1997, we had the lowest customer satisfaction scores you could imagine; customers were, in fact, angry with the company for not fulfilling its commitments to support their practices.

Many of these customers had spent years preparing for FDA approval through a "Visionary Program" that allowed them to purchase the Summit system as holmium laser, in which the excimer component would be activated upon FDA approval. As leaders in their field, they spent considerable time and money visiting sites in Europe and learning how to perform the PRK procedure and manage complications. Imagine then how they felt when the company opened "Summit Centers of Excellence" staffed by inexperienced surgeons and staff as direct competition to their businesses. Summit had become a pariah in the ophthalmic surgery space across customers and noncustomers.

We eventually sold the Centers of Excellence and started doing the right things to support our customers' practices. Meanwhile, however, my phone seemed to ring constantly with customer dissatisfaction issues from the field. In most cases, the field wasn't able to provide the relevant information I needed to make a decision. I would frequently want to know their background, training, and tenure as a customer. I would also want to know their procedure volumes, service contract status, training records, and whether they owed us any money.

Generally, what ensued was a week or two of back and forth e-mails and calls to gather all this information along with an expectation that, as Vice President of Sales & Marketing, I would solve the problem! Meanwhile, the customers' dissatisfaction and the field's frustration continued to grow.

I, too, was frustrated by this activity and swirl—all from people with the best interests and intentions. We desperately needed a common problem-solving process and language!

The over-arching theme or purpose for the new process was empowerment through driving decisions down to those closest to the activity. Sales representatives were asked to call or write with:

1. a complete description of the Current State inclusive of the facts and data previously mentioned
2. a brief description of the Desired State relationship and metrics
3. a recommended set of actions to close the gap

With this new process in place, weeks of back and forth e-mails were often reduced to a single phone call in which I approved over 90% of the recommended plans! The field won through empowerment and fast action, the customer won with better, more timely solutions, and I won countless hours I could use to focus on moving our business forward.

Change Management

An overwhelming majority of Breakthrough Process team recommendations and new processes face some level of change resistance. This is natural, as the organization has been doing things a certain way for a long time, and as creatures of habit, prefer to stay the course. Underestimating this critical element can doom even the best new process, plan, or project. Successful teams anticipate and plan for potential change resistance using proven methodology.

We have enjoyed considerable success using Ishikawa's fishbone diagram—a tool that rapidly allows a team to identify root cause(s) of change resistance. This model can be utilized in a formal Breakthrough project, but I have found it equally useful in day-to-day interactions. The goal is to be proactive and purposeful to give your company the best odds of success.

Change management has become a corporate buzzword, and there are hundreds of models and approaches that make the concept seem overwhelming. The approach I outline here provides a practical and straightforward approach to this topic.

Let's take the example of a major medical device manufacturer who made a significant investment to acquire a fast-growth start-up. After the initial excitement at the close, the newly acquired business declined precipitously—60% on a run-rate basis over the first five quarters post-merger.

Throughout the five quarters of decline, the CEO and other leaders were communicating the need to change the trajectory of the newly acquired product line. In change management terms, this is a condition we refer to as naiveté akin to managing results.

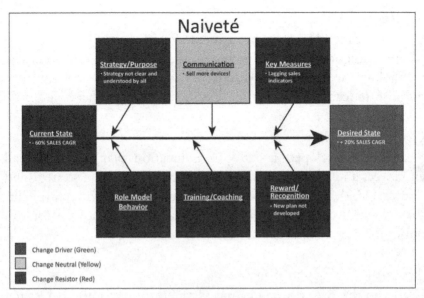

Fishbone Diagram

In reality, several change elements are holding you back. In this example, the company's **reward** (monetary) and **recognition** (monetary and nonmonetary) had not been adjusted or improved to drive to the Desired State. Likewise, **training** and ongoing **coaching** programs had not been developed or put into operation. **Key measures** were not solved, simplified, and tracked; **leaders** were not role modeling change; the **strategy and purpose** of the change was not understood by all; and finally, **communication** was considered inadequate in quality and quantity. The result, naturally, was failure.

The company formed a Breakthrough team to go deep into the Current State and identify the root cause of the decline. Several potential causes and symptoms were identified, including field turnover, account disruption, insufficient training, evolving compensation models, weakened marketing support, and inadequate corporate focus. As the team went deeper, a clear central theme emerged. The field organization didn't understand the rationale of the acquisition and how the new technology fit into their "bag." This was understandable as the start-up had been a competitor to their legacy business.

Strategy and Purpose
Understanding this gap, the team designed a new strategy—one where marketing and sales would confidently "lead" with the new technology and "follow" with legacy products. They solved the purpose, to lead the market in a specific disease state, as well.

Communication
Next, they developed a 5x5 communication plan to inform all employees and key stakeholders of the newly developed strategy and purpose. Understanding that people learn through different media, they chose five channels of communication and planned for five pulses through each over one year.

Training and Coaching
Earlier in the Breakthrough Process, the team developed a Desired State sales process. To ensure its success, they developed a world-class, hands-on training and sales rep certification program. They further ensured success by developing a coaching program for those who needed extra support.

Key Measure
At the outset of the project, myriad metrics and measures were attempted to describe the precipitous decline in sales. Using simplicity as a guiding principle, the team came up with a single metric: the number of surgeons who used two devices a week over a 90-day period. This measure of "HAWKERS" described the population for whom the new technology represented frontline therapy. The team endorsed this metric as it indicated the number of "HAWKERS" had declined from 200 at the time of the acquisition to fifty-three, allowing the Current State to be "ugly."

Role Model Behavior
The team then defined the behavior required by leaders to ensure success of the new program and process. This behavior started with strategy and communication and continued through training and coaching. In short, leadership was asked to "walk the walk" as recommended by the team.

Reward and Recognition
The team recommended changes to the Sales Commission plan to drive the new state. They also recommended a formal recognition program for teams that generated the most "HAWKERS".

Putting it all together
The team then populated and reached consensus on their initial change diagram, which highlighted the urgent need to develop a new Reward and Recognition plan.

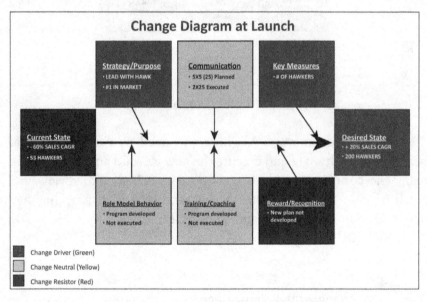

Fishbone Diagram

The team understood that the change diagram is a visually managed, active tool and that they would not accomplish the massive change required without further work. So, they pushed on over the next thirty days and revisited the diagram. They agreed they'd made significant progress, moving all Communication and Role Model Behavior to green and Reward and Recognition to yellow.

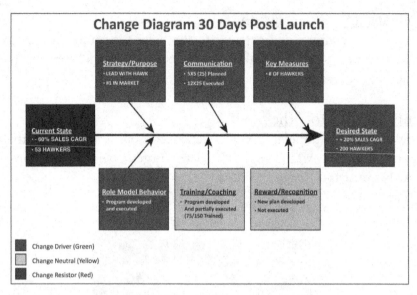

Fishbone Diagram

The refreshed diagram highlighted the need to get all 150 field personnel fully trained and execute the new Reward and Recognition plan. The continued, and 90 days post-launch met to review and reach consensus on their change diagram. In this review, they had nailed all change elements and were well on their way back to 200 "HAWKERS"!

The Results

None of the changes on their own were transformational; however, the multiplier effect associated with hitting all six elements accelerated and sustained the change necessary for this program's success.

Here is the power that each change made in the culture:

Element	Program imple-mented	Impact
Strategy and Purpose	Everyone was trained on the strategic importance of the technology.	Rather than fight the new product, sales representatives could now articulate the "why" and, as such, bought into the plan.

Communication	Enacted 5x5 communication: five messages across five channels.	All individuals were strongly aware of the program, which allowed for two-way communication of opportunities and concerns.
Key Measures	One measure identified to track progress, visibly displayed in large thermometers at all sites.	The new measure was transformational and gave an achievable and easy to understand target. This created momentum as the team saw progression.
Role Model Behavior	Leaders supported the team and removed roadblocks.	The sales and marketing team noticed the visibility and were motivated to find that their managers were behind the change.
Training/ Coaching	Reps were certified and given follow-up coaching on the process.	The quality of the implementation was consistent and led to improved results.
Rewards/Recognition	Sales commission plan and recognition tied to the new measure.	By having a clear program, the reps understood the benefit and were motivated to succeed.

<u>Bottom line:</u> While not easy, the implementation and active management of these elements worked together to drive buy-in and execution of a new process. When managing the environment rather than shoving programs down people's throats, you will position your organization to achieve rapid, authentic, and durable change.

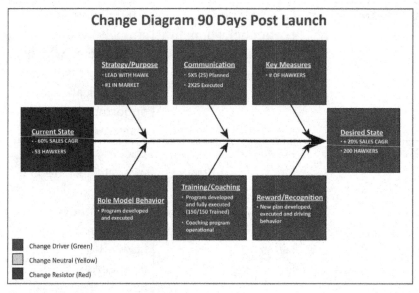

Fishbone Diagram

A few closing thoughts on applying this tool:

1. We recommend its application within the Breakthrough Process to test the quality of your initial plan and its execution.
2. It should be an active tool as the project is managed and applied at regular intervals (e.g. quarterly).
3. Red, yellow, and green levels should be discussed and agreed upon at the team level.
4. Countermeasures should be applied to all Yellow and Red vectors.
5. In the new virtual environment, this exercise can be accomplished via a simple online survey (see below example).
6. This tool can be used in any change situation within organizations, groups, and at the individual level as well as externally with customers and other key stakeholders.
7. Like many HPMS elements, the key is to use it; once you've applied it once or twice, you will get the hang of it and benefit from its power.
8. For larger projects, especially those with expected change resistance, I recommend quarterly deployment and associated corrective action through to project completion.

 **Haffey&Co.**

Change Management Survey Example

1.　The strategic purpose, intent and business rationale associated with the Desired State is clear and understood by all affected functions, individuals and key stakeholders.

- ○ Totally Agree
- ○ Agree
- ○ Neutral
- ○ Disagree
- ○ Totally Disagree

2.　A communication plan to ensure all affected functions, individuals and key stakeholders are informed of the project goals and team progress toward the Desired State is in place and operational.

- ○ Totally Agree
- ○ Agree
- ○ Neutral
- ○ Disagree
- ○ Totally Disagree

3.　The key measures of time, quality and cost to manage the project to the Desired State have been developed and are understood by all affected functions, individuals and key stakeholders.

- ○ Totally Agree
- ○ Agree
- ○ Neutral
- ○ Disagree
- ○ Totally Disagree

4.   Reward and recognition plans have been developed and are operational to support achievement of the Desired State.

○ Totally Agree
○ Agree
○ Neutral
○ Disagree
○ Totally Disagree

5.   Training and ongoing coaching plans on needed process(es), policies and procedures are operational and in support of the Desired State.

○ Totally Agree
○ Agree
○ Neutral
○ Disagree
○ Totally Disagree

6.   Role model behavior in support of the Desired State is exhibited by all affected functions, individuals and key stakeholders.

○ Totally Agree
○ Agree
○ Neutral
○ Disagree
○ Totally Disagree

CHAPTER 9

GETTING STARTED

Let's imagine that you've come out of a workshop with the first version of your organization's Corporate Success Tree, selected passionate Breakthrough Process team leaders for each of the Vital Few and are ready to start your HPMS journey. This chapter will guide you through the next steps based on best practices garnered over the last two decades practicing and teaching the system.

1. <u>Select or appoint an executive-level HPMS owner</u>
In many cases, this individual will step up and ask for the responsibility. They will likely have a background in Lean, engineering, or science and "get it" reflexively. While the CEO or "person who sits in the corner of the building" has shown his or her full support for HPMS, it's generally the support of their number two or three that drives ultimate success. I like to think of it like this: If the CEO is 100% committed to the system, this individual is 110% committed. Evidence supports the importance of this dynamic in creating a movement where, ultimately, all in the organization are passionately engaged.

2. <u>Don't let perfection get in the way of "good enough"</u>
As a student, scientist, and aspiring leader, I was trained to solve for or close 100% of the items in a given plan. When Dick Palermo first mentioned this phrase to me in December 1997, it didn't immediately make sense. It felt like he was saying it was okay to be a little sloppy or careless in our work.

As I learned more and went through my transformation, I learned the power of this statement. It starts with the fact that you've built a closed-loop management system based on strict prioritization—one where you are solving for the $\cong 20\%$ of the items that close $\cong 80\%$ of an identified gap. This allows focus and breakthrough performance on a smaller number of initiatives. Knowing the system is closed-looped (measure—improve), there will be a new Pareto based on new measures. So, if any key item is missed in the first cycle, it will likely get picked up in the second. Understanding this provides the confidence to not let perfect get in the way of good enough.

You are building a new system with new language and methodology. Naturally, it will feel a bit clunky at first, and there will be significant opportunities for improvement along the way. If you wait until you think the system is perfect, you will never get started! Most clients refresh their top-level or Corporate Success Tree on a six-month cycle to ensure continuous improvement of strategy toward the goal of perfection.

3.   Eliminate Waste

Most organizations and systems are burdened by nonvalue-added waste in the form of committees and meetings, and conflicting processes, plans, programs, and procedures. It's absolutely critical that you identify these nonvalue-added activities and eliminate them to create the space for your company's HPMS to be successful. If you bolt HPMS on top of all the existing processes, it's doomed to fail. Many will see it as "another brick in the backpack" rather than as a new, liberating, and empowering approach to getting things done.

Process mapping can be a helpful tool to identify waste, rework, delays, and constraints in your Current State. As you build your Desired State system, move the focus from inspection to support and to "less is more." Also, look for linkages and simplification of related processes, such as performance reviews. In a Lean system, these should be driven from the Success Tree, not from the typical MBO type process. You should also look at activities and events that consume significant time and lean out these processes. One that comes up frequently is board meeting preparation. Some companies spend weeks of senior management time preparing for these quarterly events—what a waste! With HPMS, I like to say we can have a board meeting anytime, in real time through your Tree and updated Stoplight Report. Invite Breakthrough teams to present at board meetings, which will further reinforce your commitment to HPMS.

Given how difficult it is to get people to change behavior and to stop doing certain things, we've found the development of an "Unsuccess Tree" to be a valuable exercise for some clients. The Unsuccess Tree can be printed on the back of your Success Tree and should indicate the activities, processes, and projects that a) you are not doing now or in the foreseeable future, and b) those that are on hold for a specified period of time.

4.   Retain a proven consultant or guide

As a product manager responsible for the Operating Room segment of Hewlett-Packard's Medical Products Group, I learned a great deal about Coronary Artery Bypass Graft (CABG) surgery. I could recite each step from anesthesia through closure. However, you wouldn't want me as your surgeon. In many businesses, especially turnarounds, your business is just like a patient. Each is unique and unlike anything you've read in a book, and when the chest is open, you want an experienced consultant or guide to assist in the operation.

5.   Consider a phased HPMS roll-out

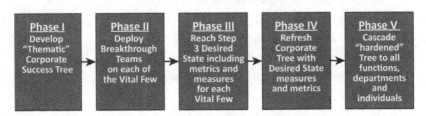

Phased Roll-Out

I strongly recommend a phased approach along these lines for the following reasons:

1. You will not overwhelm your organization by hitting them with all HPMS elements at once.
2. Following clear strategy, you will empower teams to come back to you with their Desired State goals.
3. You will reduce re-work in the cascade process.

5.   Program a six-month implementation road map.

For those interested in going on your own, here is a practical, step-by-step view of a typical first year of implementation.

Two months before the program launch:

1) Get executive-level champions onboard and select an HPMS owner (see section below). A properly educated and engaged leadership team will save you months of slow progress. Each should understand their responsibilities in promoting the system, supporting the Vital Few, and cascading it throughout their organization.

2) Review governance processes: identify redundant meetings and processes ahead of the workshop to prevent confusion.

3) Collect inputs from your stakeholders: conducting surveys and analysis can take weeks, so ensure plans are in place to have this data available ahead of the workshop.

4) Define participants to attend the first workshop.

Two weeks before program launch

1) Review all inputs to the meeting. Consider providing preread materials to all participants.

Conduct first Success Tree workshop

1) Develop the Corporate Tree.

2) Select Vital Few leaders and sponsors.

One week post-launch

1) Begin stoplight reporting.

2) Finalize team process for Vital Few.

3) Complete and review goal cascade of the senior leadership team.

4) Communicate the Success Tree to all employees; follow up with each senior leader sharing their support.

Six weeks post-launch

1) Review and approve the first round of Vital Few proposals.

2) Complete and coach cascading throughout the organization. We recommend that the leaders walk around and sample their employees to check for understanding.

Three months post-launch

1) Conduct an executive check-in on progress toward the various elements of the stoplight process.

2) Communicate progress to employees.

Six months post-launch

1) Refresh the Success Tree through a similar process as before but will include report-outs and recommendations from the Vital Few teams.

Tracking progress

Achieving full-system maturity generally takes eighteen to thirty-six months, though the team should find meaningful results within the first year. While every engagement is unique, here is a rubric to track your progress in the first year. Because each element takes effort to implement, it is common to have an organization have a mix of poor, satisfactory, and excellent items. It's most important that the leadership team identifies and improves on the items most critical to the business.

Progress check at one year

Element	Poor progress	Satisfactory progress	Excellent progress
Vital Few	Projects struggled to identify and execute breakthroughs. Few examples of meaningful benefits.	Some wins from the Vital Few projects. Leaders generally satisfied with the path forward and value derived from the projects.	Many examples of wins, and the organization has fundamentally created a compelling path forward into year two.
Stoplight Reporting	Seen as an administrative exercise. People continue to hide the real status until a major problem emerges.	Important decisions are being made at the meeting, and leaders have a clear view of progress on the Vital Few and can have candid conversations.	The Stoplight meeting is the most important meeting at the company, with engaged leaders supporting the Vital Few.

Cascading	Goal-setting using the trees is seen as an administrative exercise. Some departments have not even cascaded, taking a "wait and see" approach, expecting this system to go away	Most employees (90%+) have their trees and can articulate their top goals and how they fit into the company's success. Some still struggle to create effective goals or find daily benefit.	Employees use their trees with others to align on important projects. The organization has demonstrated significant value through improved execution and reduced project load.
Mission, Vision, and Values	These elements are mostly window dressing. Very few examples of these are being utilized effectively. Leaders have not adopted them.	Some great examples of these elements being put into practice. Leaders utilize them frequently but not at lower levels.	Many examples of use in decisions and driving the culture. Use is deep within the organization.

Failure Points

By now you've read about the power and efficiency of the HPMS through many successful examples. You may be convinced of its effectiveness and thinking through adoption at your organization. You may also wonder when and how it can fail. While the system touts simplicity, it is not easy; numerous failure points can impede success. This chapter will review the most common to consider as you embark on your HPMS journey.

1. Failure to get the right people and talent on the bus

In chapter four, I wrote about the importance of having great people on your leadership team. This chapter precedes others for a specific reason: Great People + Great System = Great Results. If you don't have great people, the best management system in the world will not produce results.

For successful HPMS adoption, your leaders must fully support and role model the system every day. They must understand management theory, especially the value of culture. One of the most powerful theories within HPMS is that Motivated Employees lead to Delighted Customers that lead to more business and Shareholder Satisfaction. This theory, which has been repeatedly proven, requires a leader to shift his or her focus from results (e.g., what you sold yesterday and how much profit you made) to the key leading indicators of customer and employee satisfaction.

Leaders who do not understand or completely buy-in to this theory end up managing or manufacturing results, many times at a high cost and lower quality (e.g., discounted sales at the end of the quarter). I have seen this behavior too often across too many companies and believe it's one of the biggest wastes in business today. These leaders think they are doing a good job inspecting and inspecting, which frustrates the worker and impedes progress. They do not understand that their role is to build great processes for their workers and support and improve rather than inspect those processes.

These results-focused leaders need to leave their old beliefs behind and embrace a new way of thinking and operating. Deming referred to this as transformation at the individual level; he also noted that this transformation was discontinuous, as if a light bulb went on. When this happens, it's a beautiful thing to see and something I've had the pleasure of witnessing in hundreds of leaders. The opposite of beautiful is change resistance, which often presents as "It's too simple" or "Yeah, but we are different." I encourage you to rapidly separate these types of leaders from your organization.

In one engagement we encountered a number two who did not embrace or utilize the system, despite the CEO's enthusiasm for and commitment to HPMS. Rather, he undermined and dismissed it in his meetings and interactions with others. The integrity of the system was damaged, people began to use the system as window dressing. No progress was made until this person was removed from the organization. Tony Hsieh, former CEO of Zappos, believes that an incorrect hire at the leadership level costs $100 million. Here, I believe that was true as Vital Few were not executed, and there was irreparable damage to the culture and confidence of the employees.

It's okay to debate and disagree on the way you want to build your system and regarding your Vital Few. Once decided, however, all leaders must commit. At Amazon, they call this "disagree and commit."

Amazon also believes in a continuously improving talent pool, which they largely achieve by continuing to raise the bar in their hiring process (e.g., ask for a writing sample during the interview). I admired and tried to practice Jack Welch's method of going through your organization with a "weed puller in one hand and a can of fertilizer in the other." Jack was trained as a chemical engineer and understood statistics. Applied to people in groups over a hundred, Jack knew they would normally distribute around average ($\cong$70% of the population).

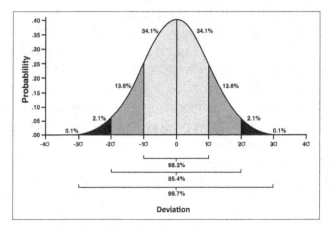

Normal Distribution (+/- 4 sigma)

He further understood that $\cong$15% of his employees were below average and $\cong$15% of his employees were above average (+/- 1 sigma). From this, he derived a process through which managers were asked to rank their bottom 10% for immediate improvement or termination and top 10% for advancement. In this way, Jack continually improved GE's talent, which was a key factor in achieving the best-in-world $400 billion increase in shareholder value under his watch. Regardless of the extent to which you buy-in to this distribution and Jack's 10%, you should have the courage to continually improve your talent. As a leader, I believed the separation number should be 3% to 9% with a corresponding high potential group of 3% to 9%.

Bottom line: make adoption mandatory for your senior leaders and continually develop your talent pool to give your organization the best chance of success.

2. Failure to Focus

Organizations that successfully adopt HPMS focus intensely on their Vital Few, invariably at the expense of the useful many. Successful project leaders and managers understand and exercise structured problem-solving and the Pareto principle; they do not attempt to solve for 100% of the items within an identified gap. Instead, they focus on the 20% of the items that contribute to 80% of the gap and rapidly solve them. They understand the closed-loop process and continuous improvement, which provide further confidence in their solutions. They also understand the negative impacts of scope creep and continually focus their teams and resources on the problem/opportunity as stated and agreed in step one in the Breakthrough Process.

I have seen clients build a fantastic Success Tree at their strategy session and one of the mid-level managers, empowered from the focus driven approach, asks, "So, can we drop X project to focus on these?" The leader then said something to the extent of, "No, we still have to do everything else." This answer took the energy out of the room; adding things on top of busy people's schedules is not strategy, and these groups often fail to achieve breakthroughs.

Bottom line: It is just as important to remove items as it is to add things. Driving real focus should feel painful.

3. Failure to Resource

High-performance companies allocate $\cong$ 70% of leadership time and resources to their Vital Few. This practice ensures breakthrough performance in these areas. In team process, these companies create an environment where leaders can dedicate up to 100% of their time to the effort, team members up to 50%, and sponsors up to 10%. Amazon, which as of this writing should be considered a "best" benchmark, forms dedicated cross-functional, cross-layer teams with sponsors that have decision-making authority for speed.

Generally when people think about the most successful projects they have ever executed, it is typically when they were singularly focused on the win, not doing fifty other tasks. The more people you have waking up every morning thinking about the Vital Few, the greater chance of success. While it doesn't seem affordable to some companies, it is even more wasteful to kid ourselves that we can create a true breakthrough when the whole team is only spending an hour a week to work on a pet project.

HPMS itself should have dedicated resources. We generally look for a passionate leader who owns and continues to drive the process. A general rule of thumb is one HPMS expert for every $100 million in revenue or one HPMS expert for each location globally. These resources should have skin in the game and wake up every morning dedicated to ensuring the Vital Few and overall HPMS success. Companies with these resources are far more successful and build strong accountability into the process.

Bottom line: make the tough decisions and resource your most important projects and HPMS for success.

4. Failure to Execute with Excellence

Successful organizations see projects through to ensure identified performance gaps are closed and that the future state is sustainable. These high-performance organizations have a bias toward action and iteration. Deming wrote eloquently about this practice in *Out of the Crisis.*

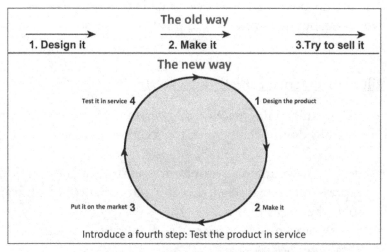

Source: Out of the Crisis, W. Edward Deming

Here you can see his penchant for simple four-step, closed-loop processes.

Organizations that execute with excellence demonstrate the discipline to track projects through until the identified performance gap is closed, regardless of the time it takes to accomplish that. They are hesitant to pick up new boulders until the first boulders are crushed. They also take the time to ensure everyone is crystal clear on the actions and who is accountable for what. For high-level leaders, this can feel painful to get into the details but necessary in organizations that haven't succeeded at executing in the past. These organizations also hold each other accountable for missed deadlines and constructively assess the root cause so it doesn't happen again.

One client had dashboards with a few red items that were not addressed. Over time, more red items appeared, just like weeds growing in a garden, until the whole dashboard was red. The system lost credibility, and the team lost morale because they did not have the focus, discipline, and resources to execute.

It's also important to iterate. Since we cannot predict the future, we will make hypotheses that may not play out as expected in the real world. Rather than continue to run an unsuccessful play, we must be willing to pivot quickly.

Bottom line: hold each other accountable for doing what you said you would do, but don't be afraid to pivot when presented with new information.

5. Failure to Practice HPMS with "Orthodoxy"

Successful organizations practice all elements of the system with orthodoxy; they do not cherry-pick tools and select elements. They:

- do not discount or overinterpret customer and employee expressed needs; instead, they drive from data to identify and solve the "right things."
- utilize proven survey science and analytics to help identify Vital Few.
- utilize facilitation to incorporate the voice of CEO/ management.
- use Mission, Vision, and Values to guide decisions and actions.
- focus as much (if not more) resources in customer and employee branch as shareholder branch (failure = overfocus on financial results).
- hold everyone mutually accountable to Values.
- fully resource HPMS and job ticket teams.
- utilize structured problem-solving where appropriate.
- hold weekly or biweekly stoplight report to track progress and intervene as leaders, where appropriate.
- utilize the change management tool to anticipate and manage resistance.
- cascade Tree to each individual and ensure they are visible in place of work.
- use time as a key measure (e.g., thirty days to initial plan).
- are willing to kill projects to ensure the Vital Few get the necessary resources.

We find that organizations that do all of the above with orthodoxy achieve a multiplier effect as some aspects of the system support other elements.

6. Failure to Solve for or Eliminate Competing Themes and Processes

Many elements of HPMS are not unique, and therefore there may be some in place when you begin your journey (e.g., Vision, Mission, problem-solving process). If these are not eliminated or incorporated into the system going forward, they create confusion and adoption challenges. We've found this to be especially true in large, matrix organizations.

In one client, we observed there were three meetings to discuss the same project. This not only drove the project leaders crazy but led to significant miscommunication. One leader used the analogy, "If you wear two wristwatches, one will always be wrong. Eventually, they removed the waste but could have saved time and energy and driven better results if they had taken the time upfront to align their systems.

Another client saw the HPMS discussions as a "plus one" rather than the most important meeting of the company. When this happens, the meeting becomes window dressing for the CEO, and the other meeting is where the projects are discussed. What a waste of time!

We recommend a careful review of the language, terms, and processes used in these organizations and attempt to lean out or incorporate these, as possible, into your HPMS.

Bottom line: be thoughtful in how and where you integrate HPMS to ensure it is the way the business is run, not a "plus one."

A High Performance Assessment

Are you curious how your company stacks up to the high performing companies highlighted in this book? If so, we encourage you to complete this simple survey.

Link: https://www.research.net/r/HighPerformanceAssessment

If you provide your email address with the survey, we will send you your results compared to best-performing benchmarks.

Copy of the High Performance Assessment

A High Performance Assessment

1. Your name:

2. Your company:

3. Our company has a concise, visible, memorable and aspirational Vision statement that guides decisions and actions.

Totally Agree   Agree   Neutral   Disagree   Totally Disagree

4. Our company has a concise, visible and memorable Mission statement that clearly answers what we do for whom, and why we do it.

Totally Agree   Agree   Neutral   Disagree   Totally Disagree

5. Our company operates through set of shared Values that result in consistent, high quality behaviours and actions necessary to achieve our Vision.

Totally Agree   Agree   Neutral   Disagree   Totally Disagree

6. Our company regularly surveys and interviews our customers to determine their level of satisfaction and to identify the top opportunities for improvement.

Totally Agree   Agree   Neutral   Disagree   Totally Disagree

7. Our company regularly surveys our employees to determine their level of satisfaction and to identify the top opportunities for improvement.

Totally Agree   Agree   Neutral   Disagree   Totally Disagree

8. Our company regularly interviews our shareholder representatives to understand their perspective on our current challenges and opportunities as well as their desired state for our company in the future.

Totally Agree   Agree   Neutral   Disagree   Totally Disagree

Another HPMS Success Story: The "HPMS Journey"

How ev3 Inc. rapidly achieved world-class customer, employee, and shareholder results

Dale Spencer, founder and chairman; Paul Buckman, CEO; and Stacy Enxing Seng, President, formed ev3 in 2001 with the goal of building a middle-market alternative to its multibillion dollar competitors in the $10 billion endovascular device market. Funded by Warburg Pincus and The Vertical Group, the team closed six acquisitions, established operations in the US, Europe, and Japan, and reached $100 million revenue by 2003.

Jim Corbett, ev3's President of International, was promoted to CEO in 2004 and successfully guided the company through an IPO in 2005. Sales continued to grow exponentially under the charismatic Corbett, exceeding $400 million in 2008. In late 2007, the company made a huge bet acquiring FoxHollow Technologies, Inc. for $780 million. This acquisition proved difficult for Corbett and his team to integrate, resulting in significant operating losses and a 40% drop in the device maker's stock by April 2008. Around this time, the board decided that a change in leadership was necessary to solve the oppbrtunity presented by the FoxHollow acquisition and regain credibility with shareholders.

The company's new CEO, Bob Palmisano, came to ev3 with a background of successfully turning companies around leveraging his High Performance Management System (HPMS). In his initial Current State analysis, Palmisano noted the presence of strong people across all functions, excellent customer relationships, and innovative products. But he noted the company was in a reactive "fire-fighting" mode and lacked a system for setting and sticking to priorities.

In his first weeks on the job, Palmisano recognized the strong leadership of Stacy Enxing Seng, President of Peripheral Vascular, and Dave Mowry, Vice President of Operations. They were sold on the value of a system and formed an enthusiastic and committed number two to help Palmisano implement the system and begin the needed process and cultural changes. HPMS spoke to Dave's background in quality, and as a result, he asked to own the system adding "HPMS" to his job title. Dave noted the pre-HPMS culture was focused on results, whereas HPMS focused on process and results, which they branded as their "Journey." The system helped break down barriers and got people to start working together. In Dave's words, it became "contagious."

While the financial pressure to perform was immense, Palmisano believed strongly in the need to focus on improving leading customer and employee satisfaction metrics. With the help of Haffey&Co., he developed and deployed satisfaction surveys to these key stakeholders. The data and facts from these surveys allowed the company to focus on a Vital Few set of priorities aimed at dramatically improving satisfaction as measured by "willingness to recommend" in these groups.

The Vital Few, along with a new Vision, Mission, and set of Shared Values, were developed in the company's first HPMS Workshop in May 2008. I was extremely fortunate to have facilitated this meeting, which resulted in the following Vision statement:

"To be the best at identifying and treating lower extremity arterial and neurovascular disease, leading with break-through technologies and process."

This simple, concise, and memorable Vision statement helped the company make decisions and guided certain actions. Notable was the absence of coronary disease—the "3" in ev3, which put a major strategic issue behind the company allowing more focus on the peripheral and neurovascular businesses. It further guided actions and investments, allowing the entire organization to lead with breakthrough technologies, namely focusing the commercial organization to re-establish the Fox Hollow acquisition to positive revenue growth and ensuring the necessary R&D and clinical investment to support the Breakthrough programs.

These elements were condensed into a one-page strategic plan, or "Tree." Leaders were urged to visibly display their

Tree and use it as a starting point for internal and external meetings. No one leaned into this aspect of the system more than Stacy Enxing Seng. Following one of her first customer presentations, in which she emphasized her Vision to be the market leader in lower extremity arterial disease, she was asked to be a keynote speaker at a medical conference focused on lower extremity disease. With this role model behavior, which she describes as "Live the Tree," she invited and included others to join her on the "Journey." Stacy, now a successful med-tech VC, felt the principles of HPMS put her in "fifth gear in my own leadership."

Brett Wall, currently EVP and President of Medtronic's Restorative Therapy Group, was another role model leader in ev3's adoption and success with HPMS. Before establishing the system and its processes, it was difficult to make decisions and, in his words, the company failed the "transparency test." Among other elements, Brett embraced the new Candor Value, through which it was considered best practice to allow the "Current State to be ugly and therefore have a real conversation about what is going on."

Brett also embraced the Vital Few framework and, for his neurovascular business, focused on generating the clinical evidence necessary to move the standard of care in acute ischemic stroke from tPA injection to the company's Solitaire™ stent-retriever thrombectomy device. This was accomplished through a $30 million investment in the multicenter, prospective, randomized SWIFT PRIME clinical trial.

Brett fiercely defended this investment through ev3's acquisition by Covidien (and later Medtronic), culminating in new AHA/ASA clinical guidelines and explosive double-digit Solitaire sales growth.

Results

Palmisano, and his leading coalition of Mowry, Enxing Seng, and Wall, practiced all elements of HPMS with enthusiasm and total commitment and rapidly achieved world-class results. On the leading indicator side, employee willingness to recommend increased from the low seventies to mid-eighties, and customers who would enthusiastically recommend the company increased from 10% to over 40%. On the lagging indicator side, ev3 recognized dramatic improvements in gross margins, profitability, and balance sheet metrics. Perhaps most telling was the 300% increase in shareholder value recognized in their acquisition by Covidien in July 2008.

CLOSING

I hope you enjoyed reading this book and are committed to developing your management system to better delight your customers, motivate your employees and satisfy your shareholders. The journey is difficult but incredibly rewarding. Each organization's journey is different and unique—only you will know which elements need to be stressed or adjusted.

Unlike the business practices of the past—where leaders commanded their teams rather than empowered them, sat in their offices looking at spreadsheets, and made things more complicated instead of simpler—HPMS helps make businesses better and more sustainable for all stakeholders.

Know that you are in good company, and I wish you the best in your journey.

ACKNOWLEDGMENTS

Richard C. Palermo, Sr.

I would like to acknowledge and recognize my mentor, Richard "Dick" Palermo, who permanently and indelibly changed my view of management by introducing me to many of the concepts in this book over twenty years ago. For that and his friendship, I will always be thankful.

> "Experience after experience indicates that there is a great need for a simple, logical, structured, balanced management system. The customers benefit from it, the employees want it, and the financial health of an organization depends on it."
>
> **—Richard C. Palermo**

Dick developed the earliest version of HPMS while serving as chief marketing officer at Xerox Corporation in the early 1990s. He later consulted with Summit Technology, where I had the pleasure of working with him from 1997 to 2000.

Throughout the sixties and seventies, Xerox was a global force in technology and business. By the time its flagship "914" copier was discontinued in 1973, it was recognized as the best-selling industrial product of all time. In 1975, after years of record revenues and profits, the company resolved an antitrust dispute with the Federal Trade Commission (FTC) through forced licensing of its entire patent portfolio, mainly to its Japanese competitors.

Within years of this decree, Japanese companies were selling copiers for less than Xerox's cost of manufacturing, with higher reliability and ease-of-use. By 1982, the company's market share had started a precipitous drop. This was the same year that David Kearns took over as CEO.

Kearns asked Dick to benchmark the Japanese and come back with recommendations on how to transform Xerox into a company more like its low-cost, high-quality Japanese competitors and less like the people-heavy, process-light organization they had become.

This journey took Dick to Professor Kaoru Ishikawa, head of the Engineering Faculty at the University of Tokyo and to two Americans, Edwards Deming and Joseph Juran, who were collaborating with Ishikawa.

Kearns and Palermo rapidly initiated several of the breakthrough concepts pioneered by Deming, Juran, and Ishikawa, namely:

- measuring quality in the Voice-of-the-Customer through monthly surveys of 55,000 Xerox equipment owners
- empowering those closest to the work with a common problem-solving process, the ability to make decisions, and the authority to directly apply correction actions
- simplifying processes to reduce cost and improve quality
- ensuring visibility of key measures

In Dick's direct area of responsibility, Business Products & Systems, he went even further. In 1985, he initiated annual employee surveys and an initial, rudimentary version of HPMS. Deming and Juran's "DNA" was embedded in these early versions, taking quality principles and practices from the factory floor to the executive suite, e.g.:

- optimizing the management system as a whole over individual functions
- focusing on the Vital Few over the Useful Many
- understanding and anticipating human change resistance to new strategies, plans, and processes

Through the implementation of this management system, Xerox succeeded in regaining lost market share at home and, by 1990, was taking business away from Canon and Ricoh in Japan. Xerox Business Products & was also recognized in 1989 with the prestigious Malcolm Baldrige National Quality Award for excellence.

The Baldrige framework, while effective, was complex and burdensome to maintain. It did, however, serve as a useful benchmark in the development of HPMS at Xerox. Over time, HPMS evolved into a simpler, more effective way to maintain and continually improve performance against the Baldrige criteria. Dick continued to develop, tune, test, and continually improve his management system as a consultant following his retirement from Xerox in 1993.[6]

Bob Palmisano

I'd like to acknowledge my good friend and mentor, Bob Palmisano, for introducing me to HPMS and for many other valuable lessons. I had the pleasure of working for and learning from Bob over the course of eight years, at two companies—Summit Technology, Inc. and IntraLase Corp.

Bob was also a big believer in the importance of best processes and HPMS in particular. I still remember December 1997 in Orlando, Florida, when Bob Palmisano and Dick Palermo introduced us to HPMS. In the same vein, Bob understood the need to properly manage, not overmanage, results. This created an environment of empowerment and support versus the micromanagement and inspection that we commonly see in business.

Lewis Baloian

I would also like to acknowledge Lewis Baloian, my consulting partner since 2016, who has helped push this management system, its processes, and our practice to new heights. Leveraging our combined thirty-five years utilizing this system across more than forty organizations and through hundreds of leadership coaching experiences, he successfully simplified and improved Dick's 8-Step Breakthrough Process™ to our leaner, more effective 4-Step Breakthrough Process™.

Lewis brainstormed and helped organize this book's contents, authored the chapter on our Breakthrough Process, and tirelessly commented on and edited the contents. Lewis' passion for what we do comes through in every client engagement, where he is universally loved and appreciated.

---

[6] https://www.nytimes.com/1992/09/03/business/japan-is-tough-but-xerox-prevails.html

I will be forever thankful for his contributions to this book, our practice, and to me as an individual as I have learned so much from him.

High Performance Leaders

I would like to thank the hundreds of managers and leaders who, over the years, have taken the leap of faith and trusted their businesses to HPMS processes and our firm.

In particular I would like to acknowledge and recognize this elite group of "High Performance" leaders who role model the system every day and, in doing so, consistently achieve breakthrough results for their customers, employees and shareholders:

Andy Corley – Bausch&Lomb, Flying L Partners
Bill Link, PhD – Versant Ventures, Flying L Partners
Brett Wall – ev3, Covidien, Medtronic
Earl Slee – ev3, Covidien, Medtronic
Eric Weinberg – InttaLase, LenSx, RxSight
Glen French – ApniCure, Asthmatx, Pulmonx
Jim Lightman – Summit Technology, IntraLase, Wright Medical, Vapotherm
Joe Army – Vapotherm
Joe Wishon - Medtronic
Joe Woody – Covidien, Acelity, Avanos
John Berdahl, MD – Vance Thompson Vision, Equinox Ophthalmic, Melt Pharmaceuticals, ExpertOpinion.md
Jonathan Talamo, MD – Mass General Hospital, Mass Eye and Ear, Harvard Medical School, Ocular Therapeutix, Johnson&Johnson Vision
K. Angela Macfarlane – ForSight Labs, Voyant Biotherapeutics
Lance Berry – Wright Medical, Vapotherm
Lisa Kudlacz – Avanos, Teleflex
Randy Alexander – Intramedics Intraocular, ReVision Optics
Rob Carson - Medtronic, Waters Corp
Ron Kurtz, MD – IntraLase, LenSx, RxSight
Scott Drake – Spectranetics, ViewRay
Sean Carney – Warburg Pincus, Hillhouse Capital, Beta Bionics
Shar Matin – Spectranetics, ViewRay, Cordis

Stacy Enxing Seng – ev3, Covidien, Lightstone Ventures
Terry Rich – Wright Medical, Alphatec Spine, Surgalign
Tom Frinzi – Bausch&Lomb, WaveTec Vision, Johnson&Johnson Vision
Vance Thompson, MD – Vance Thompson Vision
Will McGuire – Second Sight Medical Products, Ra Medical Systems

Their contributions to our experience and this book are countless. For that and the friendships we've developed along the way, I will always be grateful.

Finally I would like to thank Tom Ehrenfeld, senior editor at the Lean Enterprise Institute, for his help organizing the major themes herein and for providing motivation along the way.

ABOUT THE AUTHOR

Bernie Haffey started his professional career as a physics teacher and ice hockey coach at Delbarton School in Morristown, NJ. This early experience in teaching, science and team sports shaped much of his approach to business and many elements of this book. Upon graduation from business school, he worked as a product manager in Hewlett-Packard's Medical Products Group in Waltham, MA. He then moved to Mentor Corp, ascending from New England sales representative to Vice President of Sales and Marketing. From Mentor he moved to Summit Technology, Inc. where he assumed the role of Executive Vice President and Chief Commercial Officer through its $1 billion sale to Alcon Labs. Bernie held the same role, EVP and CCO, at Intralase Corp. through its $800 million sale to Advanced Medical Optics (now Johnson&Johnson). From there he successfully served as President and CEO of two venture-backed start-ups: NDO Surgical, Inc. and Nexis Vision. Bernie also previously served as a founding board member at WaveTec Vision, Inc. (acquired by Alcon Labs) and at Ocular Therapeutix, Inc. (NASDAQ: OCUL) and currently serves on the board of On Target Laboratories, Inc. Bernie now runs Haffey&Co., a management consulting firm that has supported more than forty organizations in implementing HPMS and achieving breakthrough results. Bernie earned a BA from Colgate University and an MBA from Cornell University.

Contact us

If you are interested in receiving expert guidance and consulting support for your company's HPMS implementation, please contact Haffey&Co. at CuttingThrough@haffeyco.com.